THE NIGHT BEFORE
THE MORNING AFTER

THE NIGHT BEFORE THE MORNING AFTER

SCOTT NEWMAN

NEW DEGREE PRESS

COPYRIGHT © 2020 SCOTT NEWMAN

All rights reserved.

THE NIGHT BEFORE THE MORNING AFTER

ISBN

978-1-63730-001-5   *Hardcover*

978-1-63676-013-1   *Kindle Ebook*

978-1-63730-000-8   *Digital Ebook*

CONTENTS

"Life moves pretty fast. If you don't stop and look around once in a while, you could miss it."

—FERRIS BUELLER

FOREWORD

———

Identifying characteristics of individuals presented in the narrative have been altered to protect their identities. Dialogue is recreated from memory. This is a true story, whatever the hell that means.

TIMELINE

———

- **1998:** Date of Arrival into this mortal world of ours

- **Summer 2012:** Antibes Round Uno (7th grade summer)

- **Summer 2013:** Antibes Round Dos (8th grade summer)

- **Fall 2013:** Commencement of the boarding school years

- **Summer 2014:** Paris go Round One (9th grade summer)

- **Summer 2015:** Paris go Round Two (10th grade summer)

- **Summer 2016:** Jordan (11th grade summer)

- **May 2017:** Graduate from Lawrenceville

- **Summer 2017:** My boss gets shot. My ass gets hauled out of the United Kingdom. Accepted to Princeton

- **September 2017:** The College Years Begin in Earnest

- **Summer 2018:** Corporate Contacts (freshmen summer)

- **Summer 2019:** Chile (sophomore summer)

CHAPTER I

SOMETHING LIKE AN INTRODUCTION

——

You know those sappy coming-of-age stories where in the end somebody reflects on all the partying and hedonistic debauchery of the past however long and waxes lyrical about how eventually the light was seen? Some version of boy meets girl who pushes him out of his own way. The guy keeps it hardcore for as long as he can, and either dies, overdoses, or breaks, and embraces change—often too late to get the girl, who, somewhere along the way, thought it best not to stick around. That's a genre. It makes sense. It sells. It rakes in the ratings. But it's a broken god-damn record.

This isn't that. It's a celebration not an apology, a raising of my glass to the cities, people, bartenders, and acrobats that have gone along on this wild ride with me for the past eight years. I won't apologize, and I shouldn't have to. It certainly isn't a nostalgic reminiscence of the glory days that slipped by. I know the glory days because I'm in them. At least I think I am.

This is a love letter, one man's account of all the delectably fun foolishness, lessons learned, and trips around the sun that have been my life. It's an ode to the carousel of women, booze, parties, actors, musicians, magic, madness, and wonder that have filled my days.

I won't bore you with the mundane, the vanilla, the Pillsbury doughboy shit. Nor will I pour you only the finest and pretend that all of this is just sunshine and rainbows and long walks along the beach. And no, I'm not trying to fill some kind of void. What a trifling cliché that would be. You're getting it all. The good, the bad, and the scary. I hope it does something for you. Maybe you'll like it. Maybe you'll hate it. Maybe it'll piss you off. I just want you to feel and to burn like the bright beautiful candle that you are.

CHAPTER II

ANTIBES

———

When I think about where to actually begin this god-damned romp of a story, the answer eludes me, because there really is no such thing as a beginning. One thing leads to another and suddenly I'm in medias res, in bed with the daughter of an Albanian mobster who wants to kill me or on a plane to France or Australia or Jordan or one of the other thirty plus countries I've visited. Or maybe I'm roaming joyfully through the streets of Florence at four o'clock in the morning on a Thursday when I should be in class, in New Jersey, listening to my history professor go on about the Battle of Culloden, or whatever the fuck else he was talking about that week.

Maybe the story should begin in New York in the throes of the storied Upper East Side (UES), in a secret corner of Dorrian's watching the Hotchkiss graduates stumble over each other doing blow and smoking cigs with the bouncer. Maybe it should be an exposé on kids behaving badly, a real-life rendition of *Gossip Girl*. Were my exploits made of the same stuff depicted in the show? Not exactly. But I certainly saw some shit. The 100XX zip codes have made themselves the gracious patron of scandalous behavior acted out by twelve to twenty-five-year-olds. The kids who went to Pinkberry and 16 Handles in sixth grade merit special mention. The Allen Stevenson and Spence and Trinity and Chapin and Nightingale and Riverdale and Fieldston, and Horace Mann crowd. We all knew each other, and we still do. But again, I digress. This won't be a hit piece on the Upper East Side. The UES certainly is a circus, but it's not one I care to write about in this piece.

This is all a long-winded way of saying that where this story really begins is in Antibes, a beautiful little beach town in the South of France in the general vicinity of Nice and Cannes. The story of how I got to Antibes in the first place is a bit murky. By seventh grade, I got fed up and properly bored with the whole American summer camp thing, and so I thought I'd venture abroad. I started looking at programs in France because my family all speaks French—

and I was learning French in school—and I figured, why the fuck not. I was fourteen at the time. Eventually, I found one called "Centre International D'Antibes"—CIA. I picked it randomly, not knowing what to expect. It was, in short, the best decision of my life.

The Antibes stories could go on for hours. I mean, I guess it's worth talking about what the fuck we were doing there in the first place. I said that I had found a program, but I gave no context as to what that actually meant. Basically, it was this French language camp where kids from all over the world descended upon this little agricultural high school campus and took French classes in the mornings from nine to twelve. In the afternoons from twelve to seven, we were free to wander around the riviera. So, of course, we drank and smoked and did whatever the fuck we damn well pleased. I remember the first cigarettes I ever purchased were from the train station in Antibes. It was a pack of Lucky Strike Vert, menthol crushables.

I remember buying large bottles of Baileys in Carrefour, clearly underage, and drinking them on the beach, as one does. I remember tasting absinthe for the first time.

When I got to Antibes, it was a crash course in how the world works. I know how ridiculous that sounds—the spoiled rich kid vacationing in France learning about the common man in the midst of other privileged teens. But it's true. In Antibes, I met kids from like thirty countries, all with a unique set of cultural norms to learn about. There were the Germans and the Austrians and the Swiss, the French and the Spanish, the Danish and the Norwegians and the Swedish and Icelandic folk, the Russians and Ukrainians, the Colombians and Brazilians and Venezuelans, the Italians and Hungarians and Estonians. It was just fucking amazing. There I was, a fourteen-year-old kid surrounded by others from all over the world.

My very first night there, I hooked up with this Russian girl. She was awesome. Then the next day, she called me her boyfriend, and I said, nah man I don't fuck with the labels because I was a cheeky fourteen-year-old excited by the prospect of sowing my oats even though I was still a virgin at the time. As a result of my rebuff, she proceeded to have her friend Igor—this enormous Ukrainian goon—come to my room, suffocate me with a pillow and hold my legs down. As Igor restrained me, she pulled an open season on my stomach and ribs, punching incessantly. She didn't break anything, but it wasn't especially pleasant. She and Igor then started laughing uproariously and poured me a shot. I guess that's how they do it in Russia. I knew from there that I had better buckle up because it was going to be an awesome fucking summer.

My god, it was a hell of a time. The loss of innocence. The realization that girls can get whatever they want, more or less, from weak-willed men. The realization that charm is a vice and a virtue that transcends culture and can get you out of pretty much any kind of trouble without exception—other than the really bad stuff. Most importantly, I learned that laughter is a language shared by all, that keeping in touch with people is an investment with exponential returns, and that at the end of the day, we really aren't all too different.

My friends and I got up to all kinds of shit. We would regularly take the train to Italy, flagrantly violate the seven o'clock in the evening check in rule, and sneak out at night. One time, on the ride back from Italy we blasted porn from our phones to the dismay of other passengers. Another time, and this is really emblematic of the Antibes experience, James, me, Alejandra, and Alejandra's friend snuck out one day, had dinner at a fancy hotel in town, took a cab to Juan Les Pins, bullshitted our way into a truly shit club called "New York" next to Le Village, raged all night, and got back at like four o'clock in the morning or something. My god, those were the best of days. That was the first time I had ever been on the inside of a nightclub. Remember again that I was fourteen. James, a big British rugby bloke, remains one of my best friends to this day.

So, of course, I returned the next year. Antibes round dos was even fucking crazier than the first. James was back too, and together we ruled the camp like self-appointed paramilitary oligarchs. It was a beautiful time. I had it figured out right good as a fifteen-year-old. I wanted to wring the juice out of life that year, and believe me, I did. I spent two staggered parts in Antibes that summer. That is to say that I went to Antibes, came back to NYC then I returned to Antibes. On my first flight to Antibes, I befriended and ended up fucking this forty-something-year-old Russian woman named Valeriya.

Once I was actually in Antibes, my friends and I broke just about every rule a person could break. At one point, I even got close to hooking up with one of the animateurs (counselors, essentially, that worked there). Another time, four of us snuck out one night by climbing over a fence in the back of the camp. We then called a taxi and took it to Cannes, whereupon we saw T-Pain perform live. I ended up hooking up with some twenty-four-year-old French lawyer, and James hooked up with both Alejandra and her friend—the fucking savage. On the car ride back, we had to pull over the car so Alejandra could yack in the light of day—maybe this was like six or seven? We were welcomed back to the camp with high fives from our friends and stern looks of disapproval from the animateurs, who had been up all night looking for us. I felt a bit bad about that, but if I could do it again, the only thing I would've done differently would have been to sneak out more often.

Antibes was full of debauchery, for sure. But it was also a crash course in how to get along with kids from all over the world. When I scroll through my three thousand-plus Facebook friends, I'd guess that between two hundred and five hundred of them are, in some way, connected to Antibes. With a degree of relative certainty, I'd say that I'll have couches to crash on almost anywhere in Europe for the foreseeable future, in large part because of the relationships I've kept up.

Beautiful. That's the only way I can describe Antibes, a beautiful little beach town where a piece of my heart shall remain forever and always.

CHAPTER III

VALERIYA

———

When I was fifteen, I fucked a forty-something-year-old Russian woman I met on an airplane named Valeriya.

Technically, actually, I met her at the airport before we boarded the plane together. And yes, it was all above board and consensual. Like you, I am—at least now—well aware of the legal grey area this puts her into. Of course, I changed the details to protect her and again reiterate that it was completely consensual. I orchestrated our encounter, and I never once felt powerless in the interaction. I know that there are those among you who will come out and lampoon this as wrong. I certainly don't identify as or feel like a victim, so let's get that out of the way up front. I'm not taking a stance on the morality of this. Nor am I trying to set an example for some weird teenage sexual fantasy. But this really happened, strange as it may seem, and I'm here to tell the god-damned story behind it.

After graduating from middle school, I did a three-or four-week stint in Antibes. Then I returned to New York to take some condensed social psychology course at Columbia. When I finished the Columbia course, I returned to Antibes.

I met Valeriya on my first flight overseas. We kept in touch and texted frequently while I was there. Upon my return to New York and the commencement of my Columbia course, we went on a few dates. Then we fucked.

Terminal Four. Gate thirty-whatever. 9:30 PM EST. The flight was, naturally, delayed, and everyone there grew more and more impatient as time whistled on by. Then I saw Valeriya standing there frustrated, so I walked over and struck up a conversation about how Delta sucks. I remember exactly what she was wearing and, frankly what I was wearing at the time. It's strange to remember such details, but I do. She had on tight jeans that were fashionably torn, a white blouse, a tailored form-fitting blazer and, of course, long, penetrating heels. I had on green J-Crew shorts, a navy Henley, a fake Rolex Daytona, and my signature jewelry (rings, bracelets, necklace).

By the time they finally started boarding like twenty or twenty-five minutes later, we found ourselves on the plane asking some stranger to switch seats so that the two of us could sit together. Throughout the flight, I labored under the distant not-so-romantic hope that, eight hours later, we would both be proud and certified members of the mile-high club. Maybe we would have even gotten our names inscribed on a little MHC plaque reserved by the airline for members who have boldly done the deed. Sadly, such events did not transpire. I did, at her behest, hold her hand during takeoff because she didn't like heights. And by flight's end, we swapped contact information and promised to meet again.

That's how it started. "Hello" goes a hell of a long way. So too does bonding over shared frustration.

I was in Antibes for two or three weeks before getting back to the city, where Valeriya and I went out on a couple of dates. For our first one, we went to Brass Monkey. She lived in deep Brooklyn—like way out there—and so she came into Manhattan with three friends and got there before I did. I'd been three or four times and knew the bouncer and the bartender, but there was a new guy at the door. Fifteen-year-old me didn't think anything of it because I'd been there a bunch of times. I handed him my ID and into his pocket it went, putting a damper on the night before it even began.

Embarrassed, I texted Valeriya telling her that they had taken my fake ID. She and her two other Russian friends came out, and one of them, this tall blonde woman with six-inch Louboutins argued vigorously with the bouncer saying "give me ID" in a heavy Russian accent like twenty times. The whole spectacle was really very silly but also kind of hilarious. There stood me, Valeriya, and her other friend—all decked out in high heels and leather jackets and looking very, very Russian—next to a blonde woman demanding that a bouncer return a fake ID that was not hers to me, somebody she'd never even met. Standing there, on the other side of the Boom Boom Room and Le Bain (which, at that time still had a certain social caché and panache to them), I couldn't help but smile. It was a big smiling mess. It was absurd that this was happening. But it was.

As our trip to Brass Monkey was shanked in the ass by a silly little drinking law, we got a table at The Standard's ground-floor restaurant. Perched on Little West 12th street and sandwiched between Brass Monkey on the left and Le Bain, a club with a hot tub on the dance floor, on the right, The Standard is as swanky as they come. So, it was fitting that I was there with a group of over-aged cake-faced Russians who smoked Marlborough Golds because, of course they did. We chatted about life and Zen and their careers and boyfriends and the rest. Frankly, I felt like I was an intimate member of some elite book club. And every now and then, the Russians made sure to plop in unsolicited life advice about this or that or whatever.

That night I tried foie gras for the first time because one of the Russians was using her boyfriend's black card to fund the feast. Frankly, the foie gras was terrible. I wasn't then nor am I now any particular fan of the prized ceremonial dish. Caviar, on the other hand, especially when it's put on pizza, I hear is delicious. Nobody really likes foie gras though. They eat it solely because it's expensive. Very similar to people who wear Gucci. It was an out of body Holden Caulfield experience. Was I really on a date with three single forty-something Russian women? Yes, in fact, I was.

For our next date, she had me meet her at some Italian restaurant off Emmons Avenue in deep, deep Brooklyn. This place took me a solid hour and sixteen minutes to find. We dined and chatted, and I made up some elaborate fairy tale about how I won my Rolex from an underground poker game in Monaco. The watch, I'll be the first to admit, was about as real as the story about how I procured it. In terms of replicas though, it was one of the best I'd ever seen. Bought straight from the source in Thailand. Some real Rudy Kurniawan shit.

After eating, we went to some cute little seaside bar in Manhattan Beach. I told her I didn't want kids, not that I had any plans of impregnating her. She told me that she liked them in theory but that in reality they seemed like a bunch of whiney little shits. How romantic. We stayed up late, drank too much, and soon it was well past midnight. When I announced I was ready to take the subway home, she deplored the choice and insisted that I take a ride home from her guy. Not that I was suspicious of "her guy," but I didn't want to pay an $100+ fee for a simple trip into Manhattan. It wasn't a chauffeur, you see. It was just some limousine service that drove Europeans and Russians around in Lincoln town cars. I told her I'd take the car, got the number, then left promptly for the Subway.

For our third and final date, we went to some French restaurant on the Upper East Side. Valeriya was joined that night by her friend, who spent most of the evening flirting aggressively with the waiter, despite having a rough around the edges, sixty-year-old boyfriend. Translate: sugar daddy. So, I couldn't really blame her for her flirtations. She probably had an itch that Mr. Rotund-around-the-waistline simply couldn't scratch.

After that, we went to a hotel in midtown that I had booked using Hotwire.com. She had told me a few times some story about how one of her best friends and her boyfriend liked to hookup in hotels because they thought it was kinky. So, I took a page out of their playbook and on into some generic Marriott we strolled.

I had to use a fake ID to check in because they typically don't rent hotels to adolescents, but, in order to avoid the Brass Monkey affair round dos, I checked in early that afternoon to avoid a scene. I also left condoms in the safe. Safety first, kids! Gotta cover up the monkey before you get funky. Wear a raincoat. Wrap. It. Up. A child is, by far, the worst and most expensive STD a person can get.

The rest, more or less, is history. One funny detail I remember about the story is that, as she was riding me, her phone rang, and I answered it. Confused at what sounded like an angry Russian woman screaming into the receiver, I later learned that the woman on the other end of the line was Valeriya's mother. I shouldn't have answered the phone, but I thought it would be funny if I did. And, to be fair, she didn't dismount. In fact, she continued rocking back and forth and even put her hand over my mouth so that I would be quiet while she conversed with her mother. She didn't seem to mind that I was balls deep inside of her. When she hung up the phone, she told me it was her mother, and we both just started laughing.

The laugh turned into an orchestral moan that echoed through the night, straight into the ears of Dr. T.J. Eckleburg. I can still hear the steady thump of her breasts as she lunged forwards then receded—that rhythmic symphony that reminded me just how lucky I was to be with this beautiful woman.

Again, please don't take this as pandering for high fives and back-slaps from the boys. The moral of this story, not that I fancy myself a poor man's Aesop, is that "hello" goes a hell of a long way.

CHAPTER IV

KATHERINE BLACK

———

I first met Katherine Black at precisely the same time that I was seeing Valeriya—during my stint at the Bogotá of Morningside Heights that separated two rounds of delectably fun foolishness in Antibes.

Beautiful and sincere, witty and unflinching, angry and excited, Katherine was Nirvana incarnate. A Cobain-inspired teenage rocker with a hell of a lot of swagger, a quick wit, and looks to kill. I never believed in love at first sight until I met her. Sometimes you just know. You can fall in love for a minute or a month or a decade. It's still love, even if its fleeting. When I see a beautiful woman walk by and I don't say hello, consequently losing her forever, it breaks my precious heart. This wasn't the case with Katherine.

She probably saw me ripping cigs between classes, or maybe I took notice of her Mötley Crüe tee.

"Hi, I'm Scott and you're the most beautiful girl I have ever met."

She swears that I stopped after "Scott." My eyes must have expressed then what my larynx could not.

She cut straight through the bullshit and that was probably why I liked her so very much. There was no need for the hello's or how-are-you's, the what-do-you-do's, the where-are-you-from's, the do-you-come-here-often's. No need to ask about her scars or tattoos or faded mascara, or slowly dissipating red nail polish. No need to inquire about how, despite the tight leather jeans and faded moto jacket atop an acid-wash Mötley Crüe tee, she held it together like some Victorian aristocrat. How she smoked like a chimney as I did. Or how she forced a smile despite the shit she had seen.

We both loved The Peppers and The Impressionists and Bukowski and watching conversations from a distance while imagining what was being discussed. This most often resulted in our making fun of random, unknowing victims. It was childish and cute and utterly adolescent. But it was our thing. The roast sessions we had were nothing short of legend.

Though this is an ex-post-facto roast about one of the academics we encountered at Morningside Heights' little Cartagena, I can say with certainty that this is precisely the kind of Mad-Libs inspired roast up with which Katherine and I would've come up with, directed specifically at one of our professors:

"This scruffy bearded motherfucker epitomized what it meant to be a soy boy. Short and stout like one of Snow White's overgrown dwarfs, he was a vegan, of course, and smoked rolled American Spirits. He probably had mangled, unkempt pubes and fucked his girlfriend exclusively in missionary exactly 3.5 times a week, using an especially thick condom that he lathered in extra lubricant. Despite his copiously delivered cunnilingus, his partner likely refused to reciprocate, a reality he accepted not long after they had begun their relationship. (Who can blame her!). He likely drove a Prius, peed sitting down, and masturbated to porn with trigger warnings."

Hopefully that gives you a taste of her wit and wisdom. This girl did not give a single solitary fuck. We took that course and got on well and everything was dandy and wonderful—as things tend to be when you're young and exited and curious. As we tooted our horns and danced our dance, the summer slipped through us like a pack at a music festival. All the while, life roared ahead around us as the busy marching of eight million fiery souls raced towards something cold, elusive, intangible.

As the sun ran in circles and I thanked my lucky stars for Katherine and tried to hold onto her while I could, I fucked Valeriya, went back to Antibes, and quickly fell through the beat-to-shit floor of Webster Hall and into freshmen orientation at boarding school.

Days turned into weeks and weeks into months and months into a year, and we lost touch because that's just how life goes—shifting gears, she has a distinctly unpleasant knack for leaving me with a face full of exhaust as I shrank in her rear-view mirror. What we had was something that once was, or that might have been, if only I'd stayed or gone or done something differently.

I did get in touch with her eventually though. She'd booked it to California, westward in search of the American dream. She hadn't notified or consulted me in anyway, and, at the time, I was furious and confused and terribly, terribly sad. I felt that I was owed some kind of explanation—even a five-minute sketch she did in the subway or a postcard or *something*.

She was sixteen at the time of her departure, just about ready to say goodbye to adolescence forever and for aye. So, she headed West in truly American fashion: Lewis and Clarke, Manifest Destiny, Freddy T's Frontier Thesis. She wasn't alone. Her Thoreau-inspired affair afforded her good company.

She's a painter by the way. For all I know, she headed out yonder to become the next Frederic Church.

Our relationship never hit the physical plane. We never even kissed. Maybe she was just *a* or maybe even *the* girl that got away. Nonetheless, I'm fairly certain that I loved her.

It's only now that I realize my love for Katherine Black didn't really have anything to do with her at all. To this day, I couldn't tell you very much about her. She was more than just a pretty face, but our emotional connection was a mile wide and an inch deep. She was an idea. Katherine Black *was* love. Sappy as it is, I suppose, then, that I was in love with the idea of love.

As I near the end of my drink and this piece, typing furiously and hoping to send this off to my editor before the sun comes up, I'm confronted with the irony that often tends to con its way into the party of my life. What I mean is that I continue to love her. I dream about her often, and she pulls me through those sleepless nights that writers tend to have—even if she, Katherine Black, is only but an idea.

CHAPTER V

THE BOARDING SCHOOL YEARS

———

After two bouts of bliss-filled chicanery in Antibes coupled with the Katherine Black run-in and the Valeriya affair, I found myself sitting around in what seemed like group-therapy and waxing lyrical about *Shakuntala, The Catcher in the Rye, The Great Gatsby, Macbeth,* and all those other books and plays that over-excited, over-educated English teachers love to talk about. [1,2,3]

It was an adjustment, to say the least. I went from running around the Riviera to sitting around a large ovular table with a bunch of teenage virgins and suburban kids who thought Molly was someone's name, that a bump was a type of greeting, and that sex was all exciting and mysterious.

———

1   Kālidāsa, and Ashok Sinha, Shakuntala: A Play on the Birth of Bharat (Bloomington, IN: Xlibris, 2011), n.p.

2   Jerome David Salinger, *The Catcher in the Rye* (Harmondsworth: Penguin Books, 2019), n.p.

3   William Shakespeare, Jesse M. Lander, and Kevin Stanton, *Macbeth* (New York: Sterling Signature, 2012), n.p.

I know I may sound like a dick here. It's not like I was some ever-experienced guru in the company of millennial innocents. I had just seen a lot more than they had—of people and of the world. I'm referring almost exclusively here to the preppies, the kids from rich suburbs like Chestnut Hill, Greenwich, and pretty much anywhere in Virginia and central Jersey. The kids who bootstrapped their way into Lawrenceville and got scholarships and grew up with a real struggle, that's another story. Who the fuck was I to judge them?

I certainly wasn't one of those kids. If anything, I fell more into the silver spoon camp than the bootstrapping camp. I'll be the first to admit that I have been extremely fortunate. I create a lot of opportunities for myself, and I am a headstrong little go-getter, but I still stand on the shoulders of giants. Birth lottery, living in New York—the whole thing.

There were the classic boarding school stories, to be sure. Kids sneaking off to the graveyard or the music building or the golf course to hookup or smoke weed, sticking alcohol in Gatorade bottles, all of it. They used to drug test kids who'd gotten caught. One hilarious example from my day involved one kid buying fake piss from another and carrying it in an unraveled condom to the health center for his urine test. He ended up dropping the piss-filled condom in front of the nurse on his way to the bathroom. Another time, this crazy kid planted alcohol in another kid's room in an attempt to cause him to lose the election for dorm president.

The girls would eat their cheerios and peanut butter. The boys would watch *Blue Mountain State* and pretend to be frat bros. They'd play lacrosse and hockey and football even if they were trash and quote Thad Castle. They'd be rude to the girls, and the girls would intentionally dumb themselves down in order to play the stereotype of what they thought the boys would like.

Don't get me wrong, it was an amazing school, and I'm humbly grateful for having been given the opportunity to go there. But in the end, I never really belonged there, and it set me down a destructive path. Do I regret it? That's tough to say. One thing leads to another and that inevitably becomes your life. I probably don't regret going. But I do regret what I did there. Or more specifically, what I didn't.

My four years at the Ville were a crazy journey. As a II former (a freshman), I had this absolutely loony English teacher, Marta Vollera. She had these eight rules for class that I'll always remember.

1. **Be Shockingly Brilliant**

2. **Be Wildly Creative**

3. **Take Risks**

4. **Tell the Radical Truth**

5. **Fall Passionately in Love**

6. **Suspend your Disbelief**

7. **Have Fun**

8. **Be Outrageous**

She encouraged us to let our freak flags fly and to put out whatever ideas we had. She even directed her Fiction Seminar class to run around campus with chalk and write whatever they wanted on buildings. She once told us about a "hookup" that had happened in her classroom the previous night by announcing that a cleaning crew had been in there minutes before we sat down.

As a side note, there was something called the "Harkness Club" at Lawrenceville wherein, by graduation, students would try to hook up on a Harkness table.

She told us all kinds of wild, unrelated, superbly interesting stories. Instead of reading *The Odyssey*, she had us memorize the preamble and recite it before every class. The recitation was unfailingly accompanied by wild theatrics that included marker throwing and jumping up on the table.

She had her own method of doing things, and she was the living embodiment of not giving a single solitary fuck.

Then there was Topher. He was the other naughty grandparent. That is quite literally how Marta and Topher referred to themselves. The naughty god-damned grandparents. Topher was a big man, in size and personality. He was loud. He was Southern. He was strongly opinionated. And he taught all kinds of unrelated classes simply because he was well-read and could. From the Arab-Israeli conflict to the story of the universe to world religions, the man lectured about whatever he damn well pleased.

I'll always remember the Jenna story. On one of the first days of class, Topher announced that we were going to have to write book reports on "pleasure reading" throughout the year. As he passed a sheet of notebook paper around the classroom, he asked us to write down the name of the book we were currently reading. Now, I could have written anything.

I planned on doing most of those book reports based off of the SparkNotes anyway. I could've done the book I had just finished or the book I was planning on plowing through next. But I didn't.

So as ink bled onto that innocent piece of II form notebook paper from Alexa Hilden's notebook, the title appeared: *How to Make Love like a Porn Star*. It was Jenna Jameson's biography, coauthored with Neil Strauss—the dude who wrote the books on pickup artists, Marilyn Manson, and Mötley Crüe. All the other padawans in the class giggled and snickered. And I was, of course, smug and satisfied with the attention I had garnered. Needless to say, Topher reprimanded me after class. I started in with a case for why I should be allowed to write a book report on a self-made entrepreneurial young woman who bootstrapped her way to success and epitomized a modern-day version of the American dream. He was having none of it and immediately shut that shit down. That was Lawrenceville year one, the one when I was free and unhampered.

By the time I got there, Lawrenceville was already on the other side of unwarranted generational change. Hazing, larrikinism, debauchery, pranks and all of that were pretty much eviscerated. It was by no means draconian. But it was soft, an unfortunate by-product of leftist, feel-good, participation-trophies ideology. To give but one simple example, there used to be a tradition where we went out in the middle of the night and every kid got a cigar and a bottle of champagne that they had to finish by dawn.

By the time I got there at the start of the second decade of this fucked up twenty-first century of ours, the champagne had been replaced by sparkling cider, and there were no cigars to be found. Kids used to fight and beat each other up. They used to drink in their dorms and slap each other on the back. They used to sneak out and take trains to New York. They used to rabble rouse. That kind of shit doesn't happen anymore because, well, I don't really know. It just doesn't.

What I am convinced of is that kids should be allowed to be kids and fuck up sometimes without dire consequences. But in this world of college admissions and selectivity and competition out the fucking wazoo, kids can't be kids. I certainly couldn't be a kid, which brings me to the next crucial exploratory element of my Lawrenceville experience.

In high school, by choice and design, I had no friends. None. I was friendly with people, sure, but I woke up one morning early my sophomore year and decided that I wanted to go to a top school, which in my head was Harvard (H), Yale (Y), Princeton (P), or Stanford (S). Early on, I read *How to Be a High School Superstar* by this dude Cal Newport.[4] The protein was essentially that doing shit that was hard to explain was better for the admissions process than doing shit that was hard to do. Frankly, most of it involved really devoting yourself to all kinds of progressive save-the-world initiatives, which I did in stride. The colleges ate that shit up like cereal.

My singular goal was getting into a college with a single digit acceptance rate, and so the extracurriculars began. I applied to everything. Every club. Every leadership position. Everything. I mean, for fuck's sake, I don't know how I had time for all of it. I ran the Interfaith Initiative and sat on the Diversity Council. I was a staff writer and a senior columnist for *The Lawrence*, the co-Editor-in-Chief of *The Lawrenceville*

---

4   Cal Newport, *How to Be a High School Superstar: A Revolutionary Plan to Get into College by Standing out (without Burning Out)* (New York: Broadway Books, 2010), n.p.

Historical Review, a contributor to *The Lit* (our school's literary magazine), and a Mock Trial participant. I also co-founded and ran a news publication called *The Contour* with two other girls. We had an editorial board of twelve kids from ten countries, covered four regions (Africa, the Middle East, East Asia, and Latin America), and in 2016, we got the Courage in Journalism Award from Youth Journalism International.

My summers were all spent resume padding in one way or another. Over the first two summers, I lived in Paris taking classes on French cuisine, cinema, and the Enlightenment. I also took a creative writing class at The Paris American Academy with a bunch of people ten to twenty years older than me. In my third year, I got a scholarship to study in Jordan, where I learned Arabic. On top of all this shit, I was an academic powerhouse. I pulled straight A's and rarely ever let the blemish of a minus molest the right side of the letter. I think when all was said and done, I graduated *Cum Laude* with a 3.8.

All of this, of course came at a price. I spent every Saturday night in my room for three years doing homework or studying or working on my extracurricular's. And they were cool. But they were all undertaken with the express purpose of launching me into H, Y, P, or S. I never really pursued what I loved. I never took the time to even try and figure out what that was. I robbed myself of the adolescent high school experience I could've have gotten. That experience was part of why I left the city in the first place. And yet, I still managed to elude it. There was no time for thinking and no time to stop. I never questioned why I was doing any of this shit, I just did it.

I regret not making friends. I regret not taking sports seriously and getting the experience of really being a part of a team. I regret skipping birthdays and plays, school dances and social events, and I regret keeping my nose so fucking clean. There's something about breaking the rules—or at least taking some kind of risk—that bonds people together. I didn't drink. I didn't hook up. I didn't even so much as vape. It wasn't worth it. I had a vision: H, Y, P, or S, and there was nothing I would let happen to jeopardize that. More than anything, I regret not getting into any trouble.

In some ways, I led two lives. In Paris and Antibes, I was a free-wheeling wild child. As a sixteen and seventeen-year-old, I lived in Paris on my own, hooking up with significantly older foreign goddesses, drinking sailors under the table, and living like a king. It was fun, unpredictable, and controllably out of control. People loved me, and I loved life. I loved living on my own and figuring things out, as one does. In Jordan, I learned Arabic and feasted on Iftars and managed to get myself lost in the Great Rift Valley and found by a group of angry Bedouins.

I skied too. I skied all over the world, and that was always my refuge. Skiing is graceful and lovely, a retreat in and of itself. Of course, there's a difference between cutting through groomed trails and hitting the back country, but I always enjoyed both. Boxing and ballet, together in unison on the mountain. Almost nobody at school knew about my other lives. The ones where I raced against the trains.

In the end, I did get into Princeton. I won the game I was playing. But it wasn't free. As important as it is to plan for the future, and as virtuous as ambition may be, it's okay to stop and smell the proverbial roses. I ran through my sophomore, junior, and senior years of high school without skipping a beat. I was *on,* always, and I put the whole stock of my existence into an arbitrary end.

There was no good reason for it. There was nothing tangible I hoped to achieve by attending an Ivy League school with a single digit acceptance rate. Part of it might have been vanity. More than anything, I think it was just an arbitrary choice. It's a hell of a lot easier to pick something, anything, and use it as your green light, your North star, than it is to wonder haplessly through life taking things as they come. The uncertainty of a future unknown is too great a burden for most to bear. At least it was for me.

There's something to be said about smelling the roses though. As the leading twentieth century humanist and philosopher Ferris Bueller once so eloquently put it: "Life moves pretty fast. You don't stop and look around once in a while, you could miss it."[5]

---

5   *Ferris Bueller's Day Off*, directed by John Hughes, Paramount
     Pictures, 1986.

CHAPTER VI

MR. BOLLINGER

———

"If you can make one heap of all your winnings
And risk it on one turn of pitch-and-toss,
And lose, and start again at your beginnings
And never breathe a word about your loss;
[...]
Yours is the Earth and everything that's in it,
And—which is more—you'll be a Man, my son!"

-*RUDYARD KIPLING*[6]

The only real friend I had at Lawrenceville was James F. Bollinger. The man was seventy-something-years-old and used to liberally drop the most brilliant aphorisms, quotes, and anecdotes into all of our conversations. At the end of our last class each semester, he would stand up and recite a line that Brutus delivers to Cassius at the end of Shakespeare's *Julius Caesar*: "forever and farewell," he'd remark triumphantly, "If we do meet again, why, we shall smile; if not, why then, this parting was well made."[7] He wore

---

6   Rudyard Kipling, "If," c1895.

7   William Shakespeare, John Gilbert, and Ned Halley, *Julius Ceasar*, complete & unabridged. ed. (London: Macmillan Collector's Library, 2016), n.p.

a tweed blazer to class every day, smoked cigars, drank whiskey, wrote in cursive and carried on a tradition of scholarship that was admirable, tried and true. He was very old-fashioned, accepting only paper copies of our essays and marking them by hand. He wore cowboy boots and expensive watches, and he was the baseball coach for as long as time can remember.

Of all the anecdotes and aphorisms, witty puns and hilarious sidebars, the story Jimmy chose to share that resonated most and has had the biggest impact on my life pertains to the motorcycle man. You'll have to forgive me if I don't get all of the details right, but Bollinger told us once about a man he knew well who, out of his love for a girl, made the grand trek across the continental United States from California to Georgia because she was there. 2,300 miles. Innumerable cigarette cartons, Lays bags, gas station runs, and long nights later, he made it to the diner where she worked, whereupon he learned that, in fact, she had been talking about him to her coworkers all summer. He was so close. Almost there. He had, after all, made it to Georgia. He quit his job to chase this girl by the way, and she was damn near ready to leave her job at the diner for him. And he came to her. And her coworkers told him that he had just missed her, but that if he hustled, he could surprise her at home before she went to bed.

Then, he was hit by a driver—a sober one—who sped away. Like a blown-out candle, he was vanquished from the face of the earth, never to breathe, love, be loved, or to toast again. The life was ripped from him violently like a plant not yet ready to leave the earth, its roots still clinging forcefully, deeply, and with great strength to the innermost pipes of the soil.

The whole thing was senseless and sad. 2,300 miles and he could've been knocked off his bike by wind, trucks, cars, or anything else God threw his way. 2,300 miles and he could've died ever so easily. And yet, as she pulled into her driveway that night, he laid lifeless, face down, and forgotten in the middle of a crosswalk. Like a flame, he was there and then, suddenly, he wasn't.

Bollinger gave the twenty-three-year-old's eulogy and assured us that was the first serious piece of writing he ever had to do in his life.

> "Ladies and gentlemen, I am not so foolish as to think that you all are going to become writers. I know most of you hate writing. I don't care. You're here because one day you're going to need to write something that matters, as I once did. I'm going to see to it that when that day comes, you get it right the first time because believe me when I tell you, life will not give you too many second chances."

He was right. About the writing and about life. The story sticks with me to this day because it's an earnest and heartbreaking reminder that we're all headed towards the same inevitable demise. Life itself can be violently ripped out of us anywhere, anytime, depending on how the winds blow. We don't have to be riding motorcycles or skydiving or swimming with sharks. This guy was crossing the bloody street. So, live it up. Make like Nike and just fucking do it. Don't wait until tomorrow to start whatever it is you wish to commence. Talk to that girl. I certainly can't control the hungry clocks that devour my life. I can control how I fill my days, and how willing I am to take after Rudyard Kipling and risk it all on a game of pitch and toss.[8]

---

8   Kipling, Rudyard, "If," c1895.

CHAPTER VII

PARIS

———

The summers of 2014 and 2015 were some of the most formative in my life. Full of magic, madness and wonder, they left golden scars on my heart that will remain there solemnly for the rest of my breathing days. In some ways, I'm still there. Because you can't ever really leave the place. Paris was a dream. A great big beautiful dream where nothing and everything seemed real. It was a cocktail party full of acrobats masquerading as people and people masquerading as acrobats who never stopped dancing. Paris for me never really existed. It was something of a hallucination.

In 2014, the summer after my freshmen year at Lawrenceville, I moved there for the summer. Shacked up in Pigalle in the heart of the red light district, I took a bunch of classes with a program called Education First (EF). Nominally, the classes were designed to teach French. As I was rather proficient already though, I got to take a bunch of cool electives like French cuisine, French cinema, Parisian studies and all that kind of stuff. I probably learned a thing or two, but I skipped a large portion of my classes in favor of more leisurely pursuits. I was also the youngest one in the program. Almost all of my peers were university-aged students. It was

Antibes all over again. EF had assembled a crew of rabble rousers looking to get drunk, get laid, and explore the city of light on someone else's dime under the guise of learning a foreign language. I was no exception.

The people I met there were Belgian and Columbian, Thai and Mexican, German and American, among others. It was a hell of a combination. I was sixteen at the time.

When 2015 rolled around, I found myself back in the City of Light, this go-round taking a course on the French Enlightenment at the Sorbonne and doing a creative writing workshop at The Paris American Academy (PAA) with travel writer Rolf Potts, novelists John Biguenet and Laura van den Berg, and writer Dinah Lenney. As with EF, at PAA I was by far the youngest participant. Most of my contemporaries were well into their twenties and thirties.

Living alone in the red light district in the heart of Montmartre, I certainly saw some shit. Above all else, I learned that we're all alone in this world. We can rely on nobody and nothing other than our own will, determination, and persistence. Our boy Henry David was right with all his reliance bullshit, which wasn't all bullshit. At sixteen, I moved to a foreign country with no supervision and figured it out with grace, poise, and pleasure.

While I had friends, I took most of my meals alone, ritualistically, almost. Among others, my favorite places were Café Marly by Musée du Louvre and La Closerie des Lilas all the way on the tail end of an interminable stretch known commonly as the Boulevard St. Michel or St. Miche for short. La Closerie des Lilas is, perhaps, the best upscale bar in the entire world. The waiters wear waistcoats, white jackets, and expertly knotted bow ties. There's live piano music, and they serve exquisitely crunchy peanuts and potato chips. The place is old and storied, full of Hemingway's many ghosts and Fitzgerald's prodigal children.

One time, at La Closerie des Lilas, the bartender asked as I was nursing an old fashioned if I was eighteen.

"No," I responded, baffling him and holding out for a good four and a half seconds to build suspense and watch his heart sink into his chest before popping back up again. "I'm twenty-two."

He quickly apologized, blushed, and scurried off to take another order. I was sixteen, and he must have known it. But it was better for both of us to let it slide. People often understand each other regardless of what is said. Words, oftentimes, are nothing more than abstractions—sound waves devoid of meaning.

Over more old fashions than an old man like me can remember or a young man like the guy I was at the bar could count, I met one or two Parisians, but nothing ever really came of those conversations. Frankly, my French wasn't good enough to flirt. I could speak, but I couldn't joust. There's a fine and profoundly important difference—much like the line between bourbon and scotch. Bourbon will get it done, but not with the elegance, panache, and smooth-cruise flippity-flack that scotch will. I'm a single-malt man myself. But at the bar, talking to those girls, I was a Knob fucking Creek.

Paris is really how I came to appreciate, to love, and ultimately to depend on the bar. It wasn't just about learning to hold liquor, though that was certainly valuable. It was about learning how the world works. How men flirt. How women respond. How women flirt. How men respond. How packs of guys interact with each other and with girls and vice versa. This was Europe, so the bravado was a lot less cock-and-balls and much more suit and cigarettes. Funny how wherever you go, though, some things never change.

We're tribal fucking animals living in times for which we're not adapted. We love groupishness and yet, we know that at the end of the day we're alone, on our own in the world. There's no tribe to return to, which creates a kind of weird pent-up energy and a great deal of frustration, especially in men.

I sat. I drank. I observed. I saw how the grown-ups behaved, and I learned to lube myself up and slip in and out of groups and conversations and plots and schemes and life—like a voluptuous French cougar in a black-lace slip.

I think what really drove home the whole individualism thing for me—the idea that we're all alone and can't count on anybody but ourselves was the story of Domenica Walter Guillaume—a woman who'd out Niccolò Machiavelli himself. She may or may not have killed husbands, altered wills, manipulated ruthlessly, and got it fucking done. She knew what she had to do, and she gave new meaning to the phrase "using any means necessary." In the end, through cunning and wit, charm and flirtation, but most of all through sheer unfettered determination, she held onto a billion dollar art collection.

The headline summary of a 2010 Vanity Fair article entitled "Crimes of the Art" gets it right:

> "Behind the dazzling, billion-dollar modern-art collection—Cézannes, Picassos, Renoirs, Matisses, and Modiglianis—in the Louvre's Musée de l'Orangerie lies a scandal that rocked France's culturati in 1959 with its sensational charges of attempted murder, blackmail, and forgery, among other crimes."[9]

---

9   John Richardson, "CRIMES OF THE ART," *Vanity Fair*, April 5, 2012, n.p, accessed October 1, 2020.

Domenica was a firebrand, a boat against the current, and a master of deception, intrigue, politics, and playing the man.

On some level, she was all of us. We're all a bunch of sick Machiavellian fucks; and while we can lambast it all we want, it's a hell of a lot easier to accept that that's the way the world works.

We lost our tribes a long time ago. And now, despite the pretenses of god, country, and football, we're just a bunch of lost and lonely souls.

The second most important thing I learned in Paris relates to the importance of travel. Rolf Potts, the aforementioned travel writer who supervised my Paris round two writing workshop, wrote a book called *Vagabonding*, and he really, really hit it out of the park.[10] In this day and age, anybody can travel, even if only to the next town over. I was and remain extremely fortunate to be able to jet set all over the world. I'm not so arrogant and naïve as to believe that everybody can just pack their bags and head to the airport. Anybody can get on a bike or a bus though. Anybody can walk.

What's the point of seeing new things? I think at the end of the day, you hear a lot of bullshit. "I did eat, pray, love and discovered myself." Nobody fucking discovers themselves. Your "self"—what you like, who you want to be, how you want to act and dress and walk and talk—are constantly evolving. The importance of travel isn't to "discover" your true self. It's to figure out who you want to be. You remove yourself from your present circumstances, and you see how other people live: how they eat, how they talk, how they love, and how

---

10   Rolf Potts, *Vagabonding: An Uncommon Guide to the Art of Long-term World Travel*, 2016 ed. (New York: Ballantine Books, 2016), n.p.

they thrive. And you pick up pieces that you like here and there until eventually you build yourself, your life, and your lifestyle choices into something that you like. You don't get that by staying in your corner of the woods. For those who really can't travel at all, books and movies and poems can fill a large part of the void.

To that end, just as travel is important, so is trying something new. My first summer in Paris, I spent far more time than was advisable or appropriate hanging around in Montmartre and Pigalle, a cesspool of depravity. Pigalle, for those who don't know, is the rough-and-tumble red light district of Paris, and Montmartre, at least at one time, was a Bohemian hangout for all the artists, the underworld, and everyone in between. At sixteen, I had no business there. But I wanted to live and to learn. So, I did. The first night of my second summer, I went to a masquerade ball at the Palace of Versailles. It was a pain in the ass to get to, but once I did, I suddenly found myself alone in a crowd of thousands in a foreign country. I met some middle-aged American women, and we danced until the sun barreled over us, at which point breakfast was served, before a line of taxis drove everybody home.

I tried writing in Paris for the first time. I realize how ridiculously lucky I was to have a city like that for what could be called "inspiration." But I did. And with that inspiration, I ran to the ends of the earth, writing every day and finishing my first, currently unpublished, novel—not this one. More than anything else, writing that little bastard proved to me that maybe I could do something with my writing. That maybe it was real, not just a Hank Moody-inspired horseshit romantic pipe dream.

There's no real way to conclude a chapter about Paris because Paris isn't a city or even a temporal space in the history of my life. It's an ongoing lucid dream, a city of magic, madness, and wonder.

Hipsters overcrowd Brooklyn. Overzealous status-obsessed teens flood the Ivy League. Attention thirsters take to TikTok. Artists go to Paris.

CHAPTER VIII

HANNA

———

"For of all sad words of tongue or pen, The saddest
are these: 'It might have been!'"

-JOHN GREENLEAF WHITTIER[11]

The Hanna story is a difficult one to tell because, frankly, I don't even know if it is a story. Hanna and I only knew each other for a grand total of about twelve hours and we didn't hook up. So maybe she had that whole girl-that-got-away thing going for her in my head, and maybe that's why I liked her so much. No, without mincing words, I'll just come out and say it: I loved her. I did, I think, at least for a time as a confused and fun-loving seventeen-year-old kid in Paris with a lot of heart and not that much head.

We met during that second fateful summer in the City of Light, the one in which I was taking the creative writing class at The Paris American Academy. I met Hanna through one of the other girls in the program, a South Carolinian belle named Lindsay who brought Hanna to one of our wine nights by the Seine.

———

11   John Greenleaf Whittier, "Maud Muller," 1856.

Half Italian and half Puerto-Rican, Hanna was a real stunner with all the spunky charm in the world. She was tan, really tan, and had a head full of beautiful gold curls that she'd chopped off real short, just below the cheeks. Short hair doesn't become certain people. She was not one of those. She had a tall, slender physique and a hell of a lot of charisma all tucked behind a tight, golden smile. She was care-free, fun, and knew how to throw down. Of course, a lot of this is speculation. Remember, I only knew this girl for, like, a day.

It all started when Lindsay announced that she would be bringing Hanna out with us that night. At the time, I was, at seventeen, the youngest in a creative writing workshop filled with twenty, thirty, and forty somethings, Lindsay among them. We often went out together for lunch and dinner, sometimes for drinks too. That particular night, we had elected to hit up the Seine for one of those good old-fashioned Parisian picnics filled with wine, cigarettes, laughter, and the ripples of a thousand hungry hearts. We stopped at a grocery store to buy prosciutto, sausage, cheese, grapes, crackers, and wine. We definitely bought a lot of wine that night. Then, on towards the Seine we marched with confidence, wonder, and the peculiar nostalgia that Americans have a habit of swinging around as they gallop through the quiet streets of a Parisian night.

We got there, did our talking and hanging out, and eventually Hanna and I found ourselves engrossed in conversation. In stages, the others either left, wondered off to another spot, or got wrapped up in their own discussions. So, there we were, in Paris, on a beautiful summer evening, talking about everything from cars and girls and relationships and marriage to our respective travels around the world and keeping up long-distance friendships. We talked about art and music and mused about Domenica Guillaume—the cold-hearted mastermind who stole something like one billion dollars worth of art from three husbands, all of whom she killed. Her collection is now the Musée de l'Orangerie in Paris. She got off scot-free by forking over the collection in exchange for exoneration. A small price to pay for murder three times around, I guess. But she did it.

We talked about the time that Hanna had spent in Dubai and what it was like growing up half Italian and half Puerto Rican. We talked about Paris. And for the most part, we just sat there under the great white stars of the bohemian night and enjoyed each other's company.

When the sun finally gave in and set around elven or twelve or whenever it did, we stayed there for a while longer and probably drank more wine. Then, she had a brilliant idea and asked me if I knew where we could go dancing, and rather than go to some trashy club filled with leather jackets and pomade-clad hair, I brought her to one of my favorite jazz clubs in the Latin Quarter called Le Caveau de la Huchette, a small cozy little underground joint with live tunes and good vibes on Rue de la Huchette. There's a very small hallway upstairs with an overcrowded bar, and then you go downstairs where there's a stage for the band and a floor for dancing.

We danced the night away, twirling and spinning and having a splendiferous time. She must've been close to double my age—probably in the twenty-eight to thirty-one range, but it didn't really matter and didn't stop us from dancing. So, we danced. We danced, and we danced, and we danced until we were exhausted and probably stupid drunk from all the wine and liquor we had pounded back—damn, could she drink! She really, really could. She had an extraordinary tolerance for alcohol. I mean it was really extraordinary. I could barely keep up with her!

Eventually, we gave each other a big hug and promised to meetup the next night, her last in town. We touched base in the morning about it and she said she was game but that she had to see what her schedule looked like. And I sent her a message around eight o'clock in the evening and then another around ten. No response. I was stupidly exhausted from the night before because I had stayed up all night with her and then spent a whole day doing classes, and I think I went to a museum or something that afternoon. My habit of drinking casually during the day probably didn't aid in matters. And at 10:00 p.m. on the dot, cell phone in hand—by golly I must've looked like Gatsby hanging around in a swimming pool waiting to get a call from Daisy Fay—I crashed and slept for like eight hours. I woke up to daylight creeping in and a message time stamped at 10:16 p.m. to the effect of "Hey, sorry my phone was dead. Just saw these. Would love to meet up. Where shall we convene?" But it was too late. I texted and asked her to get breakfast, but she was already packing and soon thereafter was on her way to the airport for a 10:00 a.m. flight, and I had missed it.

Would we have slept together? Probably, but that's entirely beside the point. I really just wanted to enjoy another Parisian night with her.

After that, I never saw her again. We both lived in New York, of course, but worlds apart. She was a working woman, a bartender and a hustler on the grind. I was a teenager from the Upper East Side (a good hour-and-a-half from her by train), and I spent most of my time at a boarding school in New Jersey. We tried to make plans a number of times, but I was either at boarding school or in Jordan or *something*. There was always something.

I still haven't seen her since France. The last time we exchanged WhatsApp messages was 2016. I reached out to wish her a happy birthday last year, and she sent me a long response explaining that she had booked it out to the West Coast to escape the fear and loathing of New York just like Katherine Black, and to raise a beautiful baby girl. She's got a long-term boyfriend now who's a part of that kid's life. And I'm sure that she's an amazing mother.

We would've danced a beautiful dance, I'm sure. But we didn't. And I'm still a bit sad about that. Who knows what would've happened if we'd had that second night together? It's not like the sex would have bonded us together forever. On the other hand, a second night hanging out with somebody really does give you the chance to get to know them. Maybe we would've jumped in the fountains, ran through the streets, and had a bunch of stories to tell. Or maybe nothing would've happened. Maybe we would've ended up hating each other. I doubt that would be the case, but it is of course in the realm of possibility, as all things are.

CHAPTER IX

AN ANGRY BEDOUIN AND THE WARM JORDANIAN SUN

———

The summer after my junior year at Lawrenceville, I managed to get myself lost in the sandstone valley of south Jordan's Wadi Rum—a rift locals call The Valley of the Moon. Having successfully bullshitted my way into a government-funded scholarship program that sends adolescent Americans abroad to countries of strategic interest in the hope that they later join the state department, I packed my bags and jetted off with all the might and energy in the world. Very quickly, I found myself steeped in Jordanian culture, Falafel, and a history richer than any red velvet cake I've ever tried.

During the week, I spent my time in an Arabic crash course, the kind designed for diplomats. It was hella intense, but it was good for learning. I've lost a lot of my language skills now seeing as it's been four fucking years since I was there, but I still remember a few words every now and then.

On weekends we did all kinds of cool trips, which brings us to the subject of this particular little story. Sometime in July of 2016, we ventured off to Petra and Wadi Rum, whereupon I managed to get myself lost in the insufferable heat of a Jordanian dessert.

On little sleep and an underwhelmingly mediocre breakfast-buffet that definitely wasn't worth eight dinars, we hiked around Petra, and it was certainly beautiful. After fueling up on some good, hearty falafel, we chugged our way through the Jordanian countryside in search of Wadi Rum where, upon our arrival, we were loaded onto makeshift benches bolted not-so-sturdily into the backs of 4x4 Toyota pickup trucks that took us way out to a small camp in no-man's land where we were to stay.

Later that afternoon, a group of people decided to climb a nearby mini-mountain to watch the sunset. The mini-mountain nearest to us, however, wasn't big enough for my taste. So, I resolved to venture north to one about a kilometer or two away.

There was something about that mountain spoke to me. It was a bit of a "fuck it" moment. I felt, at the time, that if there was anything I needed to do in life, it was to run toward and ascend that fucking mountain. And so, it came to pass that Lana, the twenty-three-year-old assistant director of the program, and I ventured off towards it.

We sprinted over to the mountain, quickly clawed our way up like spider-monkeys, and watched an absolutely gorgeous blood-orange sunset over The Valley of the Moon. Having reveled in the natural beauty for just a bit too long, however, we quickly realized that we had better descend the peak and fast before the last glimmering rays of that beloved sun had vanished. And so, though only by a hair's breadth, we did just that. By the time we got down, however, it was almost completely dark and all we could see were some far-off lights—lights which we assumed to be our camp. We were wrong.

But not only were we wrong, we were really wrong. We were so wrong, in fact, that we ran into just about the last person on the planet who we wanted to see. When we finally got to the far-off lights, more specifically, there stood Ahmed. Who was Ahmed? The short answer is that he was the last person in all of Jordan that I wanted to run into. The long answer is a bit more complicated. The aforementioned state department program had been taking students to Wadi Rum for the better part of a decade. And every time they went, they booked a "hotel" with the same family. I put "hotel" in parentheses because it wasn't really a hotel. It was more like a bunch of air-conditioned glamping tents in the middle of the fucking desert surrounded by miles and miles of nothing. That year, grey flannel-wearers in the state department booked us in at what they thought was the same hotel that they had used previously. It wasn't. The ownership had changed, and it now belonged to an entirely new branch of the same family. So, we got fucked. Ankles pinned up behind the ears. The whole thing. Metaphorically, of course.

Of course, Ahmed, the guy who booked us in, didn't disclose at the time of our booking the whole ownership change situation. He played along all coy and shit. Then, the branch of the family who we usually booked with called the state department suits a few days before we were meant to come and asked why we hadn't booked with them again. Of course, it was an unanswerable question because we thought that we had. So, then we had to call Ahmed and pull thirty reservations out from under his ass so we could rebook with the other family. Naturally, this didn't please him. In fact, he and his brothers called us thirty or forty times over the period of two days. All to no avail. We ghosted him before ghosting was a thing.

Cut back to Ahmed, the angry crazy dude. With no phone, a language barrier, and an unhappy Bedouin, I was at Ahmed's mercy. He had us by the balls, and, in all likelihood, enjoyed the power that afforded him, mainly because he was pissed about the cancellation situation.

My qualms were not put to rest when he motioned for us to climb into the back of his pickup truck. This was also, of course, after a healthy dose of verbal jousting with Lana, who managed to persuade him that God had brought us together so that we could reconcile our differences.

He drove around in circles, probably to scare us. We had to change cars three or four times. Lana explained the whole situation to me in French as we bounced around the fucking trunks of three separate pickups. I had no idea where he would take me or what he would do with me, but when he motioned for me to climb into his 4x4, I had no choice but to do just that.

In the end though, we got back in one piece, and I'm alive to tell the story. Maybe it was decency. Or maybe it was some deep moral obligation he felt that he had. I think it really helped that Lana was such a champ and came up with the God bringing us together thing. In the end, I don't know why he chose to help us. It would've been pretty easy to just tell us to fuck off, which he sorta did at first. It's a cool story though. And now I've got it as a story to write about. It also makes for perfect bar banter.

On that fateful summer night in 2016, human decency transcended Ahmed's family-feud and his anger over our cancelling. Irrespective of the language barrier and our cultural differences, that day I needed help and Ahmed pulled through.

CHAPTER X

BULLETS AND BALLGAMES

—

I graduated from Lawrenceville in May 2017, and it was a grand affair filled with all the pompous, glamourous, superfluous, and perfunctory formalities that usually accompany such things as high school graduations. It was almost like an office party. Scripted. I went to prom. Even had a date. Walked across the stage, shook the headmaster's hand, graduated cum laude, finished my last semester with a 4.0, all of that. Of the colleges I'd been admitted to, I decided on Duke, and from there I really ought never to have looked back. But I did. It didn't feel right. It didn't feel fair. And for better or for worse, I still had a hell of a lot of fight left in me: H, Y, P, or S. Those were the schools that mattered. I see now how ludicrous this is, and I wish I'd had different thinking, but I didn't.

After a week or so of grad parties, I transported myself down to our beloved nation's capitol to intern for Steve Scalise, a congressman from Louisiana who also happened to be the majority whip. A real-life Frank Underwood. Whatever one thinks about politics and about Scalise in general—and frankly, at the time, I didn't think too much about the policy issues—it was objectively pretty cool to intern for the majority whip. It was just awesome exposure to see the gears of Washington DC at work as they charged forward in their perverse large-scale Tammany-Hall-esque manner of brutal forward force.

I shacked up at a swanky condo in Foggy Bottom and set the alarm for six or seven or whenever it was every morning. I'd throw on a suit, knot up a tie, and slum it into Capitol Hill where the whole charade began. The time I spent in the office, frankly, was quite interesting. I mostly had to do bitch work like answer the phones, and I wasn't paid, but it didn't really matter. It was cool to be able to see how things worked. I got to sit in on hearings and whip-team meetings. I got to meet senators and congressmen from all over the place. I got to cross paths with interns from every office on the Hill, and I got to see what a profoundly nepotistic place DC is. The only other place in the world that I've seen that level of nepotism is Los Angeles. And I'm not talking about nepotism in the classical sense of the word. It's not like senators were just appointing their children to be senate pages. But there was an enormous amount of lateral and vertical movement of the young professionals working there. They floated from office to office and moved around DC like bees: swarming, producing honey, wearing grey suits, and social climbing. There was a pervasive attraction to power. DC smells like coffee and wet ink. That's all the city is. Caffeine, newspapers, and power politics.

On June 14, 2017, I woke up to my alarm like I had every other morning for the past two weeks of my internship. I showered, did my hair and makeup—lol I didn't actually wear makeup—and began getting dressed. As I was knotting my tie, my phone buzzed. Whoever it was could wait. I was in pursuit of the perfect knot. The phone buzzed again. Then again. With my collar still popped and the perfect knot having been christened, I scooped up the little Apple device to see a weird message in the GroupMe from Jack.

"Guys, there are sentries guarding the doors to the main office, and they won't let me in. I showed them my ID card and told them I was an intern. They said no one in or out. Does anyone know what's going on?"

Jack was one of those over-achieving seer-sucker-wearing southern motherfuckers with slicked back ginger hair (probably had fire crotch to match) who liked to get there early as a bit of a suck-off gesture to the people in charge of us. So, of course, he was the first of the interns to realize something was afoot.

It was kind of creepy and bizarre that there were fucking sentries guarding the doors to the office. Then came another text.

"Guys, they're not letting anybody into the Rayburn office either. Secret service. Or security. I don't know. Guys with guns and sunglasses."

Rayburn House Office Building was the congressional district office. Our boy Steve-O was the whip. So, he had the whip's office for dealing with federal matters. And he had the district office for dealing with shit like flood insurance specific to New Orleans.

Then came the bombshell, the dropping of the proverbial hammer. A text from one of our supervisors.

"Keep this to yourselves. Please don't tell your families, but *The Hill* is about to publish a story. The boss has been shot. Stay out of the office. That's all we can share with you for now."

Fifteen excruciatingly long and warped minutes later, a notification from *The Hill* appeared on my phone with a headline that read something like: "Whip Scalise Shot on Baseball Field. Details to come."

This was right around the congressional baseball game—an annual sporting contest between Democrat and Republican lawmakers the proceeds of which went to charity. So, it made sense that he would be there at a baseball field practicing. What didn't make sense is who pulled the trigger. Turns out, ironic as it is, it was some crazy Bernie-or-bust bro who opened fire on the republicans at their practice. David Bailey, the security guy who I had met a few times in the office, was hit as well. I think there might have been a third guy too. Scalise was hit really bad though. Lots of internal bleeding. The whole shebang. It wasn't a good situation. And the guy was in the hospital, I believe, for the better part of half a year.

I was in shock and awe. What the actual fuck was going on? Was I dreaming? No, as a matter of fact, there were no dreams. Only bullets. A lot of them. Somebody had, in fact, gunned down our boy. A dark day in America.

I stayed home that day rather *shooketh* by the whole affair. We weren't allowed in the office anyway.

One of my fellow interns in the office, let's call her Sam, was a gorgeous blonde southern gal who once more or less gave me a hand job on the steps of capitol hill as well as in the backseat of an Uber after telling our Uber driver that we had just gotten engaged. She was so much fun, so light on her feet, and so quick and witty. She didn't go to the same fancy schools that I did. She wasn't from the Upper East Side. And yet, she was far smarter than any of the girls I knew from New York or Lawrenceville or would come to meet Princeton. She went to a no-name school in Louisiana, but she was still president of her class. She was ambitious to be sure. "The Bright Lights" and the "Big City," to borrow Jay McInerney's apt coining of the terms, didn't appeal to her and she wasn't awed by them. [12] She was witty and fun, cunning and cool. And she knew how to wrap men around her fingers like silly putty. She knew how to tease and manipulate, to flirt and seduce, and to do so in the way that only a social climbing professional can. She never gave away her secrets. She had these piercing blue eyes and remains one of the most gorgeous girls I've ever seen.

We hooked up once in DC, but only kissing and above the belt stuff. We were making out on my bed and she mounted me, ready to take a trip down space mountain. As she maneuvered herself gracefully on top—rubbing and grinding and sucking my neck and pressing her platinum breasts against my pectorals, she whispered quietly, slowly in my ear five words (six, technically) that I'll never forget. "See," she purred as grinded herself forcefully on top of me, "I'm just a tease." And with that, she hopped off, put her bra and shirt on and announced that we were going to see the Lincoln Memorial. "What about?"

"Oh honey," she teased. "You're just too young for me."

I was exactly eighteen months younger than her so I wasn't pleased with this, but it was what it was. So, blue-balls clad and with my tail metaphorically and literally between my legs, off to the Lincoln Memorial we scurried.

She knew how to keep a man guessing, and she applied this push-and-pull tactic in the office and her professional life too, I'm sure. There's absolutely no shame in it. She wasn't using her sexuality to advance her career. It was nothing like that. She understood how social dynamics worked. She knew how to

---

12   Jay McInerney, *Bright Lights, Big City* (London; Oxford; New York; New Delhi; Sydney: Bloomsbury, 2017), n.p.

read situations. She had strong emotional intelligence. And she could wrap weak and helpless men around her fingers like it was nothing. She had a knack for it. And I don't want to say it was a cautionary tale because she didn't do anything wrong to me. She didn't take advantage or anything like that. But she knew how to seduce, how to make you feel wanted, and how to make you feel like all the lights in the world were on you and only you.

She told me that day the day I left the internship that if I ever came to DC again, she'd fuck me. So of course, I was on a train the following week. I took it down and booked a room on one of those hotel-booking apps. The Valeryia situation incarnate. She came over. We had dinner at the restaurant in the lobby. Then we went upstairs, and we fucked. And she was fantastic at it. She was on birth control and insisted that I not use a condom. But I didn't really care to risk it, so I wore one anyway. The belt and suspenders approach. When we finished fucking at my hotel, she wanted to explore DC, and she wanted me to fuck her on the roof of her dorm. She was, at the time, staying in The George Washington University summer housing. I refused. She was upset about this. She was a wild child, a dreamer. A porn star who hadn't made her acting debut—and believe me, that's a good thing. But I was still a cub scout, and I didn't want the security cameras catching us. I was a very private person at the time. So instead of fucking on the roof we just kind of meandered around campus and enjoyed each other's company. That was Sam.

Did I love her like Hanna? No, I can't honestly say that I did. I respected her. And I admired her. And in some ways, I wanted to be her. But I don't think I could really drop the L word on her. Love is a strange and bizarre affliction that defies reason. Maybe I love her now looking back. But at the time, I didn't.

Sam and Steve. What a couple of fucking characters. And what a hell of a way to spend my time in DC. With respect to both Sam and Steve, and I write this with all due respect, I guess it's safe to say that DC went out with a bang, in more ways than one.

CHAPTER XI

CRUMPET-EATING LIMEYS

———

James Bond, Eton, Oxford, Charles Dickens, and a good cuppa. These are really the only good things to come out of England, an island nation that ruled the world for the better part of the past few hundred years. They told Napoleon to fuck off, and off he fucked. Wellington even apparently sent a grand, bizarre, and beautifully nuanced message of fuck you to the Corsican dynamo by allegedly railing one of Napoleon's mistresses. Everything else generally sucks. The food, the weather, the politics, and their border patrol agents who hauled my ass out of the country—they all suck. I say this more or less in jest. I have heaps and heaps of English friends. And, of course, I have great respect for the country. But my recent bout of fox hunting with them made me into the fox, which was profoundly irksome.

When I left my internship in Scalise's office, I had a week of downtime before jetting off to England. I used that downtime, as you know, to go down to DC and fuck Sam. When I got back from that little affair, I packed my bags and jetted over the Atlantic. Instead of strolling into Piccadilly Circus, I managed to get myself locked in a makeshift detention center with Iraqi and Syrian asylum seekers for nine hours. 32,400 seconds later, I was marched out onto the tarmac and deported from the country.

I arrived on a red-eye flight and was consequently exhausted. So, after waiting in an hour-and-a-half long line to see Mr. Customs Fucker, the cheeky cunt asked me why I was there. I told him I was there to do an internship. I assumed this was fine to say. I had deliberately gone out of the way to ask the company who I was interning with if I needed any special type of visa and they said no. I made sure to ask because this was in the middle of all that Brexit stuff. Well, they done fucked up. And I done fucked up. Because you DID need a visa. It didn't matter that it was an internship. It didn't matter that it was unpaid. It didn't matter that I showed them a ticket out for eight bloody fucking days later because I had to be in Rome that weekend for a wedding. What mattered was that I was, apparently, stealing jobs from hardworking Brits. I was caught in the crosshairs of a bureaucratic rule clearly not intended for me.

"I'm here to eat crumpets, drink tea, seduce the queen, and do an internship," I offered solemnly with a wink.

Inadvertently, I had uttered the "I" word, and the man had cum immediately in his pants. With his now stained khakis, Mr. Customers Fucker leaped into action like one of Snow White's dwarfs on a mission. This was his one chance to do something marginally interesting after a long shift of rubber stamping. So, he detained me.

Without pause, I was ushered aside to a little waiting area. Then my bags were searched, my credit cards and money counted, and my fucking toiletries rummaged through. One of these dumb fucks pulled Advil out of my bag and said: "What's this," as if he had never seen Advil before and insinuated that I was smuggling drugs into the country.

After my shit was searched, I was brought to a room where I was fingerprinted and photographed. The charade had begun. I had been sucked into the mechanisms of the state department designed policy for stopping illegal immigration.

After that, they took my phone. Then they made me sign some documents saying that I had been read my rights, and they put me in a room where I was to remain for nine fucking hours. I remember how, when I got there, the guy spoke very slowly, instructed me to sign some documents, and asked if I understood and spoke English. When I responded in the thick American accent that I did, he was startled.

Once I was stuck in this drag little detention room with diner-style tables, I came to witness who else was in there. From what I gather and what I heard, it was predominantly Syrian and Iraqi refugees seeking asylum. There was one tatted-out American guy in there crying into the payphone. He was explaining in an exasperated fashion, maybe to his mother—though I can't be sure—that he had come there to propose to his girlfriend but that they wouldn't let him in because of his criminal record. He had arranged a whole thing at a restaurant with a ring. And they wouldn't let the poor bastard in. There was another dude who was a Syrian doctor, a stand-up guy, I'm sure. But they chucked him in there with us, too, and kept him out. Then there was I. Not "me," motherfucker, but "I." The verb to be, after all, cannot take a direct object.

So here I was, in the midst of refugees who feared for their future in a foreign country whose language they did not speak. And yet, for reasons that continue to baffle me, somebody thought that it was a good idea to have the movie *Dunston Checks In* playing on the sole TV in the room.[13] For reference, *Dunston Checks In* is a film about a kid and his pet orangutan who terrorize a hotel. It's a children movie about a kid and his friend who happens to be a fucking ape. Why, on God's green earth, anybody thought that was an appropriate movie choice to be playing to refugees and asylum-seekers fearing for their future is completely beyond me. But you know what, why the fuck does anybody choose to do anything? Maybe it was an accident. Who knows?

After seven hours in there, I was interrogated. I asked the customs guy doing the interrogating what his name was to be polite. He said his name was Agent 85739. In my book, he will go down forever and always as Mr. Customs Fucker.

I explained how I wasn't taking anybody's job and how this was an unpaid two-week internship. I explained how I had tickets out of the country for eight days later because I needed to be in Rome that weekend for a wedding. I showed these tickets. I offered to fly to any other country in Europe because I saw absolutely no need to cross the Atlantic a second time. My first offer was Rome, which Mr. Customers Fucker rejected. Then I offered a procession of other random but close by cities like Paris, Antibes, Barcelona, Munich, Berlin, Malmo, Stockholm, and Oslo. All rejected. They couldn't let me fly to those places from the UK, they told me, because while I could get a visa at the border, I was not guaranteed entry. And if for whatever reason I wasn't allowed in, I would be deported to my country of origin, not the country on my passport. And my country of origin was, at that point, the U.F.K—the United Fucking Kingdom.

---

13   *Dunston Checks in*, directed by Ken Kwapis, 20th Century Fox, 1996.

So, after a little argument with Mr. Fuckhead, another less-than-patrician fuck working there, I was marched out onto the tarmac of the runway. The stairs on a plane were lowered. My passport was given to the head stewardess, and she was instructed not to return it to me until we had landed on US soil.

On my way back, I watched three movies, one of which I thought was fantastic, even if the critics—high-browed, Brooklyn-dwelling, rolled cigarette-smoking, scarf-wearing, coffee shop douches that they are—did not.

And that, my friends, is the story of how I got deported from the United Kingdom.

CHAPTER XII

HOW I GOT INTO PRINCETON

—

First, my boss got shot. Then, I got deported. Then, I got into Princeton. The year I applied, I did so in the company of 31,056 others. Of those, 1,890 (6.1%) were offered admission.[14] Somehow, through charm and finesse, I bullshitted my way in. I had dreamt of it for the better part of eighteen months. It was the validation—confirmation, really, that the past four years of slaving away incessantly and making myself into the very best, most presentable, most appealing prospective student had been for something. I was and remain an extremely goal oriented person. But I hadn't really thought through what I wanted. Harvard, Princeton, Yale, and Stanford, that's all that mattered to me. I wanted the prestige. I wanted to prove to myself and to everyone who doubted me, slept on me, and otherwise didn't encourage me, that I could do it. And I did.

---

14   Office of Communications, "Princeton offers admission to 6.1 percent of Class of 2021 applicants," Princeton University, last modified March 2, 2017.

In total, I applied to nearly two dozen colleges and was admitted to nineteen. I got into Pomona College, Princeton University, Vanderbilt University, Brown University, Williams College, The University of Virginia, Wesleyan University, Cornell University, Dartmouth College, The University of Pennsylvania, Duke University, Columbia University, Northwestern University, Washington University in St. Louis, Georgetown University, Hamilton College, Claremont McKenna College, McGill University, and Middlebury College. I was waitlisted at Harvard University and The University of Chicago. I was rejected from Yale University, Amherst College, Swarthmore College, and Stanford University.

I wasn't particularly talented or special. I was not, as they say, naturally gifted. I just knew how to work hard and to game the system. As I said, I read that book *How to Be a High School Superstar*, and the rest was history.[15] Over four years at Lawrenceville, I founded an international news publication, had a personal column in the school newspaper, ran the school's history publication, contributed to the literary publication, served on the diversity school, single-handedly ran the interfaith initiative, and was on the Mock Trial team. I did all of this while maintaining straight A's and graduating with a cumulative GPA of 3.8 at one of the best secondary schools in the country.

For better or for worse, I only wanted one thing: Harvard, Princeton, Yale, or Stanford. It consumed me. It was all that mattered. I got tunnel vision and neglected everything else in my life. To say that I neglected my relationships would be inaccurate because I didn't have any. Antibes, Paris, Jordan—that

---

15   Cal Newport, *How to Be a High School Superstar: A Revolutionary Plan to Get into College by Standing out (without Burning Out)* (New York: Broadway Books, 2010), n.p.

was all a world apart. At school I was an academic and extra-curricular weapon. I understood what I needed to do to satisfy the outrageous appetites of the admissions officers, so I got on my knees, tied up my hair, applied my lip balm, and I wrapped my lips around the large phallic farce of college admissions.

In the end, I got what I wanted. But when I look back now, I wish I hadn't sucked so hard. I wish I had made some friends, played on some sports teams, got into some trouble, and invested myself more into a wholehearted high school experience.

If there's anything I remember about the college admissions process, it was December of 2016, by far the busiest month of my entire life. On December 15, 2016, Yale deferred my application, and I was heartbroken—utterly shattered. I took a day to grieve, and then I got to work. Over the next two weeks, I pumped out twenty-three college applications—each with their own essays, short answer questions, and supplements. I got it done, but those were extremely long, extremely tense days of agony, stress knots, and pain. I frequently thought of Vin Diesel's character Dominic Toretto driving a Bugatti through two Dubai skyscrapers.[16] Once he drives it through the first one, he tries to brake but the brake plates are shot. "No *brakes*," he shouts to Paul Walker's Brian O'Connor.[17] "No Brakes!"[18] I felt like Dom in that period. Because there were no breaks and *"no brakes."* There was no time for thinking and no time to stop. I needed to pump, to churn, and to get it done. I had been so earnestly convinced that I would get

---

16   *The Fate of the Furious*, directed by F. Gary Gary, Universal Pictures, 2017.

17   Ibid., n.p.

18   Ibid., n.p.

into Yale that I couldn't conceive of not getting in. I should have gotten in, frankly, but conspiracies against me at Lawrenceville and Yale aided in the preclusion of that outcome. That, however, is a story for another time.

I remember that every night between December 15 and December 31 at around eleven, I would go to my bathroom, close the door, climb into the shower, and open the window. There's a ledge full of shampoo bottles next to it. I would move the bottles, climb on top of it, eat Milano cookies, drink a can of Guinness, and smoke a Lucky Strike—a distant reminder of the world out there. My friend Jenna—a Slovenian girl who was and remains extremely fond of me—came to New York all the way from Europe in December on her yearly trip. But I couldn't see her. I was too busy. That broke my heart a bit, but it was the discipline—the game. And as a player, I had to respect the rules.

Winter passed in a flurry of books and school, and sometime in February or March or both, I made a point of visiting both Princeton and Yale. At both schools, I emailed half a dozen professors ahead of time asking to sit in on their classes. I struck up dialogues with the ones who responded, got my ass to campus, and spoke with them at length during and after the classes. In both Jersey and New Haven, I charmed myself into the pants of these professors and got them to agree to write letters of recommendation to the admissions office for me.

After getting rejected from Yale, I wrote both Princeton (waitlist) and Harvard (waitlist) long letters explaining that while I had been admitted to some great schools, my heart lay in New Jersey/Cambridge. I felt like a whore and hated it, but the fellatio had yet to conclude. In fact, it continued into the summer.

I was being pipelined onto a highway down which I didn't want to go: the Upper East Side, boarding school, the Ivy League, Goldman Sachs, an attractive blonde wife with a wealthy father, a weekend home in the Hamptons, the right country clubs, The right social groups, the right apartment, in the right neighborhood, next to the right neighbors, on the boards of the right companies. It just seemed so fucking pre-scripted. Where was the agency, the choice? I was fortunate, extremely fortunate. But it didn't feel like the decision was mine. It felt like I was doing what I was expected to do, or at least what I thought that I was expected to do.

Eventually, I got my head out of my ass, said fuck you to prestige and the Ivy League, and chose Duke. I envisioned myself on a highway of expectations and Duke, in my view, was an exit. It was a way to get everyone and everything off my back and to start anew in Durham. I had moved past the anger of feeling cheated out of H, Y, P, or S, and I had accepted that in Raleigh, I would begin a new life.

And so, it came to pass that on June 14, 2017, Steve Scalise was shot, and I got a day off of work. And on that day off, I wrote a letter to the Princeton admissions office pleading my case. One last hurrah. One last shot at what had been my dream for longer than I cared to remember. I clicked send, and I never expected to hear from Princeton again.

The day after returning to the United States after getting deported from England, I got the call. I dropped the phone. I cried. And I could hear Hans Zimmer's scoring of the *Dark Knight* Trilogy in the background.[19] In particular, I thought of one of the last scenes from *The Dark Knight Rises* in which

---

19   The Dark Knight Rises (Soundtrack). Composed by Hans Zimmer. WaterTower Music. 2012

Alfred realizes that Bruce is still alive, that he had pulled off the ultimate con—the great theatrical illusion, the masterpiece.[20] I was Bruce. I had fooled the world, or more pointedly, the admissions office of Princeton University.

That night I took the train up to Princeton and got a room at the Peacock Inn. I walked around campus and breathed in the warm summer air. I called a classmate from Lawrenceville who was going to Princeton as well, and I told him the news. As I stood in front of Robertson Hall, I asked myself one simple question: Could I see myself here? The answer was affirmative.

---

20 *The Dark Knight Rises*, directed by Christopher Nolan, Warner Bros Pictures, 2012.

CHAPTER XIII

THE COLLEGE ESSAYS
I NEVER SUBMITTED

———

To round things out here, I'll include the college essays I never submitted. These were the real ones, the ones that actually conveyed how I felt and that best represented who I was. But the colleges probably wouldn't have been interested. They don't want genuinely interesting people anymore. All they want is some kid interested in the flavor of the day, which at the time that I was applying to colleges and dealing with this, was save-the-world pandering. The essays here are smug, angry, and aggressive. But that's partially because I resented the process of having to whore myself out. It's also the reason I didn't submit them.

I played my cards right, and, sure, I cared about the causes, but I won't do you the discourtesy of lying and saying that I devoted myself so wholeheartedly to promoting interfaith dialogue, sitting on the diversity council, working on things related to the Arab-Israeli conflict, and all that shit because I woke up and decided to save the world. I woke up and decided I wanted to go to Princeton. In the words of Walter White, "I did it for me."[21]

Here are a few essays I didn't submit but should've. Maybe next time I'll think twice about forking over my soul in exchange for the prestige orgasm I get when people began to cum in their pants after I told 'em Princeton had made a clerical error and admitted my restless ass.

I HAVE NO IDENTITY

I am nothing. I have no identity. Yes, I rub shoulders with suited penguin-looking Upper East Side aristocrats quite frequently, but I just as often spill beer on fellow Guns-N'-Roses-loving concert-goers. I love Shakespeare, but no more than I do Bukowski, and just as I fancy myself a die-hard fan of Ludwig Van Beethoven, Cobain and Eminem are certainly close seconds.

And as for the writing—a righteous old passion of mine that I've come to develop—suffice it to say that I hold an extraordinary command over narrational tone, for my stories never quite seem to be told by the same guy.

So how the hell are any of these things related, and who—more importantly—am I?

I am nobody in particular, but that's just the point. I wouldn't necessarily say that I shuffle through personas like cards, though I've certainly been accused of the trick by the occasional Strokes-loving, Harley-Quinn-looking groupie when she sees me in my own little penguin suit on the way to a luncheon of one kind or another.

Freed from the outrageous limitations of status quo conformity, I'm able to do what I love without all the

---

21 *Breaking Bad*, season 5, episode 16, "Felina," performed by Bryan Cranston, Vince Gilligan, aired September 29, 2013, on AMC.

otherwise unnecessary inhibitions with which I would otherwise have to deal.

What I love above all else, first and foremost, is to learn, and coupled with a truly relentless spirit, favorable circumstances of the academic and financial variety have allowed me to do just that. Whether it's the history of Formula One or art crimes in the twentieth century, when a field of study captures my fancy, I pursue it devoutly as a hunter does his prey. But like the fictional Harvey Specter, however, I chase goals rather than dreams—a strategy that has afforded me great success while allowing me to keep two feet on the ground and a head on these broad shoulders of mine. The pursuit of such interests as I amass, however, is never quite laborious or humdrum because I love what I'm learning—both inside of the classroom and outside of it.

Though my work around the Harkness table attempting to understand why the Met and other big private collection museums have yet to return Nazi Loot or my research into the deconstruction of Caro's Moses have certainly been interesting, I've probably learned more outside of the classroom than I have within it.

Having been fortunate to travel extensively at a young age, more specifically, I have met some truly remarkable individuals with whom I maintain epistolary correspondence to this day. I've learned just as much with a hitchhiker's thumb and a goofy smile as I have with unfettered JSTOR access, and in so doing, I've come to appreciate that all it really takes to foment a meaningful and long-lasting relationship is "Hello." Relationships really do matter, and I'm glad that I've been able to maintain so many of them through thick and thin.

Striking a similar chord, my experience with people around the world has taught me to listen earnestly, to listen for understanding rather than response, for if Seeds of Peace—a listening boot camp of sorts—taught me anything, it was that there is no right or wrong, there is only a *we* and a *they*, and without taking time to learn such a truth, conflict will persist.

Another thing that Seeds taught me—while we're on the subject—is that you can't change people by shoveling righteous-sounding rhetoric down their throats until they choke and see the error in their ways. You can't change people, and it's arrogant and misguided and silly, even, to make a valiant effort through the offering of unsolicited opinions, advice, or criticism.

And so, as the sun sets in the east, I wish to emphasize four key points about myself: I believe earnestly that hard work is the only worthwhile kind. I believe that the pursuit of learning is endless, beautiful, and ought never to be resigned. I believe that listening is an under-appreciated virtue. And finally, I believe that "hello" can go a hell of a long way.

LEARNING: A MISTRESS

I could rattle off accomplishments, accolades, and other forms of nonsensical bullshit masquerading as intellectual curiosity, but, dear reader, I guess you could say it's your lucky day, for I've humbly chosen to spare you. Rather than discuss my outrageously high grades, my ninety-nine percentile ACT score, or my long list of extracurricular pursuits and other impressive honors—all of which you can find elsewhere—I'll do half the work for you by sifting through the phony garbage and getting right down to it: I love to learn.

Indeed, I like to think of knowledge and its endless pursuit as an elusive mistress of sorts—the kind you hide from your wife and kids, of course. And so, though there's really no place to begin but anywhere, I'll share with you the story of how we met and our tumultuous journey to the ends of the earth and back.

I guess one could say that I first met her in the winds of Samsara that blow about a small beach in the old city of Antibes. Through stolen kisses, empty bottles, unfinished joints, and discarded cigarette cartons, I learned just how amazing it can be to sit with people, to listen, and to smile gently without the ambition that seems to cloud too many people's judgement these days. People from all over the world would just go to that beach, drink their drink, dance their dance, and laugh their laugh until the sabbatical our moon had so kindly granted its brother came to an all too abrupt and screeching halt with the familiar break of dawn. And as we left that beach and our conversations about the human condition, Greek gods, and everything in between, she had formed an all too tight grip on my heart and from there, I was hooked.

Through the crowded streets of Old Delhi to the worn out markets of Phenom Penn, the omnipotent beauty of Paris at night, and the familiar musk of a Harkness table, she led me on a merry little chase through travel, writing, reading, and intensive research in the library and completive soul searching in meditation. And at her command I questioned always, read in excess, and gave up never. I loved her and she seemed to love me—and that was always enough.

Surrounded by Israelis and Palestinians at Seeds of Peace ready to tear each other's throats out, I learned to listen and to make sense of all the confusion in the world. I learned of the danger that lurks behind the untruths fed ceaselessly to both sides. I learned that hate breeds hate, and I learned that the only way to solve an issue is to listen for understanding rather than response. On the soccer pitch, I learned that regardless of one's skin color or citizenship status, we're all the same teenagers with the same issues, same longing, and same love. I learned that differences ought to be celebrated rather than ostracized and that borders—as Renoir once so eloquently put it—are nothing more than man-made creations.

But it didn't end there, for having instilled in me a passion for the conflict, she dragged me through the Atlantic and across the world to Amman, where I spent this past summer learning Arabic. Indeed, the vast wonder of Petra and Wadi Rum and the shisha I smoked and Iftars on which I feasted were beautiful in their own Eastern kind of way that eludes description.

Why I chose to ignore the conventions of a typical college essay that speaks maturely about some bullshit bildungs-roman is beyond me. In fact, I've written plenty of those for my friends, and they've all gotten into their choice schools. I guess it's just that I feel uncomfortable attempting to prostitute myself to you through a polished-up version of myself. The truth is that I love to love, I hate to hate, and I have all kinds of passions which I'd like to pursue from creative writing to Formula One to law to politics to something in-between.

CHAPTER XIV

COLLEGE

———

All that glitters, sparkles, and tickles the eyes isn't gold. And don't I know it.

Let me begin by acknowledging up front as the nice young man that I am that I'm humbly grateful for the opportunity to have gone to Princeton. The professors are dope, the schooling's pretty good, and the facilities are great. But that's it. If I could do it again, I would not go there, and I wouldn't send my kids there. Princeton has changed dramatically over the years, and its changed for the worse. I should have known this of course, but I was too focused on the prestige and allure of going to the "number one" school to actually care what it would be like when I got there, and, frankly, that's on me. One thing I've learned in life is that prestige will only take you so far. *Gossip Girl*'s Chuck Bass once said to Dan Humphrey that "The world you're looking at only exists from the outside. The only reason I survive in it is that I always knew it was empty."[22] Frankly, that's Princeton. At least it has been for me.

22　*Gossip Girl*, season 3, episode 22, "Last Tango, Then Paris," directed by J. Miller Tobin, written by Josh Safran and Stephanie Savage, aired May 17, 2010, on The CW.

First off, there's an absurd pressure to pursue a career in finance, tech, or consulting. From the minute I set foot on campus, I was inundated with emails, information sessions, and the prospect of exclusive dinners and recruiting events with the top firms across these three chief industries. Finance, tech, and consulting are seen as the gold standard—the Holy Trinity. Like most kids, I didn't give any particular kind of shit about investment banking until I came to Princeton and realized that kids literally jerk off to the golden arches of Goldman Sachs. (Actually, the logo is white and blue, but you get the point). Like everyone else, I got sucked into the vortex—going to all the dinners, sending all the follow up networking emails, and taking for granted that investment banking was where I was headed. Eventually, I had the will power to pull myself out, but it wasn't easy.

The best description I've ever heard of the dilemma comes from a class of 2020 graduate:

"As the days tick by and you hear of people getting great offers and pursuing immaculate opportunities, you start to doubt yourself. You think that instead of holding different dreams maybe you're just not good enough to nail the technicalities or composed enough to handle the hours or dedicated enough to get the pres-tigious job or smart enough to think about the future.

You see your best friends who deeply care about global health or child poverty or climate change put on a suit. You see that random person that lived across the hall from you freshman year that you were too afraid to talk to put on a suit. You see the smart aleck that dominated your precept last year put on a suit. You see those people and you wonder if maybe there is something to the suit. They look good, like they know exactly what they will do with the next decade of their lives.

And you sit there and have no place to go and no job to take and you log onto Handshake and you see those opportunities. And the jobs stare at you in the face. And you're so ridiculously close to putting on a suit.

You have to consciously stop yourself from putting on a suit or else it will just form onto you. No one is immune to the suit. When something is so widespread, so deeply enmeshed in the culture of a place, you start to wonder if everyone else is clued in on something you just don't get. You start to see yourself in the suit."

Very few people, I would argue, give any particular kind of shit about investment banking. They're not doing it for the money because you can make money doing anything. They're doing it for the prestige—the ability to call themselves members of an exclusive club. That desire to get a prestige orgasm, I think, pervades all of Princeton.

From the minute you set foot on campus, you see the huddled masses scurrying around trying to get into the right student groups and societies that will lead to admission in the right eating clubs which will supposedly lead to better lives. It's not like Harvard. There, the Final Clubs actually mean something and have a weight and history and tradition that's carried on, I think. At Princeton, it's just kind of become a bit of a sad joke.

Our "top" eating club, The Ivy Club, is no longer filled with one percenters and heiresses. At least if it were, the snooty attitude of its members could be justified, or at least understood. The members of Ivy, however, are completely incongruous with the stuffy elitism the club claims to represent. So, in reality, you get a group of people who aren't very special in the real world that masquerade as elitist preppies while they're on campus. It's all just a large exercise in play pretend. And unfortunately, once the masks come on, so too do grossly overexaggerated attitudes of holier-than-though douchery that the mask-wearers sport because they falsely believe that that's how the characters they're portraying actually behave.

The same is true of The University Cottage Club. While at one point it may have been a collection of kids from powerful southern families whose company it would behoove a person to keep, now, it is dominated almost exclusively by varsity athletes from every team on campus. Cottage, however, is not nearly as bad as Ivy when it comes to playing pretend. At this point, they've pretty much embraced their athletic reputation.

Tiger Inn is full of upper middle-class kids from the suburbs who, similar to the members of Ivy, think that in order to appropriately play the character of the aristocrat they are not, they need to turn up their noses at everyone below, beneath, and beside them on the socioeconomic plane.

The Cap & Gown Club claims to be the most woke, diverse club on campus, other than maybe Terrace—where people go to smoke weed 24/7. I'll tell you this, a guy with a big dick doesn't go around constantly professing what a big dick he has. If Cap & Gown were all that woke, they wouldn't feel the need to constantly tell everybody about it.

Cannon, like Cottage, is filled with athletes, and they don't pretend to be anything else.

The club in which I briefly held membership was Cloister—a place dominated by the swimming and rowing teams.

The last of the clubs are Charter, which was for engineers but whose future is uncertain, Quad, which I think is for the marching band but don't really know, and Colonial, an establishment with which I am extremely unfamiliar.

To round it all out, you can't join eating clubs until you're a second semester sophomore so the first year and a half at Princeton is spent metaphorically felating upperclassmen. His sophomore spring, well after he had been admitted to the Cap & Gown Club, my buddy Troy was in the bathroom of the Tiger Inn taking a piss, and he saw another guy who's hat he liked.

"Nice hat bro," he offered. "What's your name?"

"What're you a freshmen?" shot back the jaded senior. It's not the best example. In fact it's a pretty minor one, but this dynamic pervades the Princeton experience.

Last year, a group of freshmen girls were found out to have made a group chat in which they traded information about Ivy Club Officers (president, vice president, and bicker chair) in the hopes that they could more easily "become friends" with influential club members.

I never took things to this extreme, but I was there doing it with the rest of them. I was no better. I kept track of all the upperclassmen I met, made lists of who I knew in each club, and tried to game the system.

Princeton, at least to a degree, made me into a social climbing weasel and it was fucking disgusting. Just like the aforementioned upperclassman said, that shit forms around you subconsciously unless you break out of it.

Related to the eating clubs is the social scene, which I have found to be extremely boring, dull, and repetitive. The parties uniformly end at two o'clock in the morning, and there's very little drug use. My buddy got banned from a club for a year for doing coke in the bathroom. It's deplorable. Nothing crazy ever happens. It's all very tame, very controlled, and very fucking boring. There are bars in Princeton, but students don't go. It's just townies.

You go to the same eating clubs twice a week every week for a whole semester. The theme nights are not taken seriously. It's just the same punch-in-punch-out routine. And you can't just show up. Any time you want to go out, you need to have a member of an eating club put you on a guest-list as there is hired security at the door. If these places were actually filled with elegant, beautiful people and celebutantes, I could understand the pretension. I've never had a problem with the kind of security measures enacted at trendy places in New York. But Ivy and Cottage are hardly Public during Fashion Week.

Another grievance I have about Princeton is the overwhelmingly leftist environment on campus. This is far deeper than merely progressive politics. The professors are by and large a bunch of full-on leftists. I asked somebody once if there were any conservatives in a particular department and was told the most right I'm going to get at Princeton is democrat. For the number one institution in the country to not have a single conservative professor is ludicrous. Conservative professors are shunned and looked down upon. There's probably only one at Princeton, and his name is Robert George. Some of his opinions are extremely controversial, and I don't agree with all of them, but that's not really the point. It's not about agreeing or not agreeing. I'm just pointing out that the number one school in the god-damned country might do well to have a little bit of diversity of opinion when it comes to who they choose to appoint.

Consider the Sokal Hoax or the more recent Sokal Squared Hoax. There's a great article in *The Atlantic* about that shit.[23] The long and the short of it is that a bunch of professors went around submitting ludicrous and intentionally outrageous papers to extremely left-leaning publications and got some of them approved and published because certain topics are so relegated to field of academic mumbo jumbo that even if they're downright silly and absurd, there's a place for them in academia.

Look at these titles, as reported in *The Atlantic* "Human Reaction to Rape Culture and Queer Performativity at Urban Dog Parks in Portland, Oregon." Then there was "Rubbing One Out: Defining Metasexual Violence of Objectification Through Nonconsensual Masturbation."[24]

My freshmen year at Princeton, I had to read portions of Lauren Berlant's book, *Cruel Optimism*, as well as chapters from this truly absurd piece by Jane Bennett called *Vibrant Matter: A Political Ecology of Things.*[25,26] To show you, my friends, the extent of the lunacy to which I'm referring, this is an excerpt from summary on the Duke University Press website:

"In *Vibrant Matter* the political theorist Jane Bennett, renowned for her work on nature, ethics, and affect, shifts her focus from the human experience of things to things themselves. Bennett argues that political theory needs to do a better job of recognizing the active participation of nonhuman forces in events. Toward that end, she theorizes a 'vital

---

23   Yascha Mounk, "What an Audacious Hoax Reveals About Academia," *The Atlantic*, October 5, 2018, n.p, accessed October 1, 2020.

24   Ibid., n.p.

25   Lauren Gail Berlant, *Cruel Optimism* (Durham: Duke University Press, 2011), n.p.

26   Jane Bennett, *Vibrant Matter: A Political Ecology of Things* (Durham: Duke University Press, 2010), n.p.

materiality' that runs through and across bodies, both human and nonhuman. Bennett explores how political analyses of public events might change were we to acknowledge that agency always emerges as the effect of ad hoc configurations of human and nonhuman forces."[27]

No, I don't know what the fuck she's talking about either. I do abstractly, but frankly, this is such academic mumbo-jumbo that I'm curious to why we were made to read it in the first place.

It would be wrong to say, as *The Atlantic* article suggests, that this is representative of all of academia.

This kind of lunacy, at least in my experience, has not made its way to Princeton, other than in a few assigned articles here and there—at least not yet. What can be said is that we're headed in that direction, and I don't like it.

There is no robust intellectual environment at Princeton. Kids aren't sitting around and excitedly talking about the things they're passionate about. Nobody talks about Plato, Socrates, Kant, and Kierkegaard. They talk about recruiting and about themselves. Not once in four years at Princeton, with the exception of some sociology junkies talking about Marx, have I heard people discussing anything intellectual. For that matter, I've rarely heard people talking excitedly about other random shit they're passionate about. Most people at Princeton, in my opinion, are extremely self-absorbed, narrow-minded, and for the most part, uninteresting.

Finally, I would just say that Princeton is far too hard. Grade deflation. Kids spending hours every day in the library. That's the norm, and nobody questions it. You don't have

---

27 Duke University Press, "Vibrant Matter A Political Ecology of Things," Duke University Press, accessed October 20, 2020, https://www.dukeupress.edu/vibrant-matter.

people throwing a frisbee around. You don't have people playing beer die on the lawn. You don't have darties. It's not a thing. People just study. All the fucking time. They study to get high GPAs that they hope will lead to jobs at Goldman Sachs. But more than that, they study because it's the only thing they know how to do. When you go to a school with a six percent acceptance rate, you get kids that don't know how to do a hell of a lot else than bury themselves in their fucking books.

This is all just to say that for all the hard work I put into getting in, the result was ultimately underwhelming. I'd be tempted to say something like: "If you're going to fight for something, fight like hell. Just make damn sure you know what it is for which you're so desperately fighting." Because, for the most part, that captures it pretty well. But I do believe in trying new things. I tried something new with Princeton. But I didn't trust my gut. My gut told me I should've gone to Duke. But instead of following it, I fell back into what I thought I was supposed to do to impress other people. So, with that, I'll end this chapter less eloquently.

Fuck everyone else and whatever it is you think that they think. Do whatever the hell you want. It's your life, not theirs.

CHAPTER XV

CORPORATE CONTACTS

———

Then there were the flirtations and foxtrots with corporate America. The summer after my freshmen year at Princeton, I contacted and met nearly 300 C-Suite (or similar) executives across industries in New York, Boston, Connecticut, Philadelphia, and DC on behalf of Business Today (BT), Princeton's largest student organization. Over twelve weeks, I raised over $200,000 from thirty-eight donors, increasing my team's revenue by twenty-five percent, becoming the largest 2018 fundraiser for BT. In addition to fiscal sponsorship, I secured participation in our events from seventeen executives (including three keynote addresses) for our International Conference, organized an on-campus event, and contributed multiple interviews to our magazine and online journal.

I guess a few words of background are necessary here. Hell, they definitely are. Here's what you need to know.

First and foremost, *Business Today* is a publication that was founded in 1968 by Steve Forbes, Michael Mimms, and Jon Perel. It started as a magazine—a kind of pro-business publication designed to defend capitalism in the era of hippies and flower girls and communes. Over the years, it grew and eventually became the "largest" organization on Princeton's campus, or so they claim.

There's also, of course, the conferences. That's what BT is best known for. They host two or three large-scale conferences every year where they fly in kids from all over the world (in 2017, they had one-hundred-and-fifty kids from eighty universities across forty-five countries) to NYC for an all-expenses paid three-day conference at the Grand Hyatt in NYC. There, they hear from tons of CEOs and executives across industries. Finally, BT brings speakers to campus and runs an online journal, which publishes weekly compared to the magazine which publishes twice a year.

Corporate Contacts (CC) is the lifeblood of Business Today. The aforementioned conferences and the magazine need to be paid for, and they need to be filled with A-list executives. That doesn't just happen. Every year, ten Princeton students spread across the US to solicit participation and sponsorships from CEOs across industries. CC Managers maintain existing relationships with past and current sponsors and are tasked with finding new ones.

My time as a CC manager affirmed for me the virtue and nobility of persistence. When I applied for Business Today my freshmen fall, I was rejected. It wasn't until the spring when I heard about CC that I gained admission. Upon my acceptance, I was told that I would have to drive. My partner had a license but refused to drive. So, I learned, taking lessons in and between my classes.

As to the actual job, I went all in and managed to increase our revenue by quite a bit in a year when each of the other CC teams—there are five—under performed. As with the college admissions thing, I wasn't necessarily smarter or better positioned to succeed. I was a workhorse, and I understood the virtues of charm, finesse, and politics. Dialogue was lyrical. It was music. And I knew how to play my instrument to the nines. So, I did.

A day in the life went a little something like this:

RISE: respond to emails, read news, read bios of executives we would be meeting later in the day, and double-check schedule.

MEETINGS: Attend three to five back-to-back meetings across town, scurrying from one to another.

PROPOSALS: Send thank you notes and sponsorship proposals to all parties met that day.

SOURCING: Spend one to three hours "sourcing" (scouring the internet, using a variety of tools, for the contact information of target sponsors). A typical sourcing session produced one-hundred leads and one-hundred email addresses. Schedule a "sequence" (a sequence of emails including an initial contact email and six pre-written follow-up emails that would send automatically until a recipient responded to a message in the chain) of one-hundred emails to be blasted out via MixMax (the Mail Merge-like software that we used) for the following morning at 6:00 a.m. I scheduled the sequences at 6:00 a.m. to give executives the false impression that I was an especially early riser. Plus, this got my message in before the flood of other emails they were likely to receive throughout the day.

FOLLOW UP: Each week, I would email follow-ups about the proposal, asking whether they accepted or declined and whether or not they had any questions, to all parties that I had met to date that hadn't yet responded. This was typically on Mondays.

On Tuesdays, I pulled out my ever-growing stack of business cards and called. If I got no response, I left a message.

I continued contacting the recipients of my "outstanding" proposals until they told me to fuck off or agreed to donate. At any given time, I would have between twenty and one hundred outstanding proposals. Typically, the number was on the lower side because I called so often that I usually got an answer.

MORE EMAILS: I never let an email sit in my inbox unanswered for more than two hours, other than between the hours of midnight and six o'clock in the morning. In this sense, I worked eighteen-hour days, six days a week.

SLEEP: There wasn't much of it, and I quickly became a caffeine and nicotine fiend. Starbucks and JUUL were integral parts of my daily fuel. Basic Bitch Box Checked. Don't @ me.

Lather. Rinse. Repeat.

It may seem drab, but whenever you go all in on something and get serious—unless its hedonism—you have to put in the hours. As romantic as it is to be a "writer," a large portion of it is parking your ass in a stool for hours at a time and forcing yourself to write.

Overall, I can say with certainty that the experience was really fucking cool. As a twenty-one-year-old, I whored myself all over the Eastern seaboard sitting in long, elegant board rooms and meeting c-level suit wearers at all kinds of companies. Among others, I met top dogs at Hermes, Breitling, Bose, Wawa, General Dynamics, Boeing, and National Geographic. There were also, of course, financial giants like Bain Capital, State Street, Wellington, AQR, and Bridgewater. There were scores and scores of other examples like this. I was a twenty-one-year-old undergraduate. I had absolutely no business waltzing confidently into conference room after conference room, shaking hands, cracking jokes, and pitching.

A wise woman once told me that the default answer to the unasked question is no. I wasn't going to take no for granted. By summer's end, I had met close to three hundred CEOs or other senior executives. Why? And more specifically, how? By asking.

Persistence was the driving force, the engine. Charm was the car itself—the thing that put the engine to work. Call it charm, finesse, or whatever you will, but I had little trouble bringing it out. Of the deals I closed, I probably spent eighty percent of the time listening earnestly, cracking jokes, and drinking in the sagely knowledge of the person on the other end of the table.

The pitch was almost an afterthought.

Within two minutes of meeting, an exec knew whether they were going to give or not. It wasn't about the organization or the cause. It was about me. Could they trust me? More importantly, did they like me? People tend to like those who listen, those who smile understandingly as Gatsby did. And it wasn't phony or Machiavellian. I really was interested. These guys were the top dogs of their bullpens. It was an absolute treat to speak with them and pick their mind. It was persistence that got me into the room. It was an interest in the other person that got me out of there with a check.

Finally, there was the issue of the aftermath. After busting my ass and becoming the largest fundraiser in a historically under-performing year where every other team drastically underperformed and didn't come close to their targets, I was fucked, given the treatment that Boxer got in *Animal Farm*.[28] My thanks and commendations were brief and fleeting. Not

---

28 George Orwell, *Animal Farm: A Fairy Story* (New York, NY: Signet Classics, 2020), n.p.

long after I returned to Princeton, I was slowly pushed out of the organization that I had single-handedly sustained. How ironic. It's often the people you help most that are the quickest and most willing to fuck you. This isn't to say that trust is bad and inevitably leads to getting cucked. But sometimes it does.

Embrace the excesses and the absolutes. Commit wholeheartedly to painting the walls with blood and tears. Throw paint on the god-damned canvas. Dare to go all in, to lose yourself, and to be extraordinary. Far better to leave it all on the field than to just sort of exist unimposingly as you're along for the ride. Whatever you do, don't be another domino like every other sad sap wearing a gray flannel suit and clocking out at the same time every day.

Sometimes, as I did, you devote yourself to the wrong thing. Not everybody or everything is worth your best efforts. Excesses and absolutes are noble, to be sure. And I'm certainly glad I pushed myself to the ends of the earth as a Corporate Contacts Manager. In the end, Business Today was, by no measure, worthy of the effort I put into it. So, I'll end with the advice I almost gave at the end of the Princeton chapter: if you're gonna fight for something, fight like hell. Just make damn sure you know exactly what it is for which you're so desperately fighting.

CHAPTER XVI

HENDRICK'S & TONIC

———

In February of my sophomore year at Princeton, I went to a recruiting event for a bank, a dinner and cocktails kind of affair. When the presentations concluded, I stuck around to mingle, network, and socialize. This, after all, was at a point in my life when the external pressures of Princeton were getting to me, and when I felt that banking was the thing to do. The power of the suit beckoned.

Completely by accident, I ended up talking to Ava, thinking that she was an analyst as well. She wasn't. She was on the investor relations team—though she called herself the CFO—chief fun officer. We immediately hit it off.

She had finished her PhD at Columbia in 2016, focusing on French and Spanish literature, a topic that was certainly lively, interesting, and thought-provocative. We traded quips about Paris, Antibes, Sartre, Camus, and the rest of the postmodern gang. That's where it all began. At a recruiting event for a bank.

I ran into her on campus about two months later when she came to meet some prominent alumni who were there for the weekend. She invited me to meetup and I, thinking it was a recruiting thing, told her I'd get back to her. I suggested coffee. She countered by offering dinner as she was only in Princeton for a few days. When I got to the restaurant and she ordered a Hendrick's and tonic, I knew that I wasn't there to be recruited.

We danced our dance for a month or two, and it was really very fun. I'd go into New York between Thursday and Sunday—sometimes just for the night, sometimes for a couple days at a time, and we'd go out to restaurants and bars and hangout in my apartment or hers.

I fondly remember getting cocktails with her at The Penrose and Ethyl's and having dinner at JG Melon's, Dono-hue's Steak House, and Elio's. We relegated much of our drink-ing to the Upper East Side. For one, I lived there so it was easier for us to go back to the apartment afterwards, and in some weird kind of way, in addition to the fact that she wasn't into the whole meatpacking thing, I didn't want to go out-out with her there or, god-forbid, take her to the Lower East Side and run into a bunch of my friends. I wanted to show her that I wasn't just another undergrad, even though I was, and that's probably part of why she liked me.

Other times, she'd come to Princeton and we would stay at the Nassau Inn, or The Peacock Inn, or some vacant Airbnb, if we were feeling adventurous. We'd go out for dinner in town, maybe hit up a bar, and then off to bed we'd retire or the activities to which we week by week looked forward to.

My thing though was this: I would never stay. We'd hook up until one, two o'clock, or later, and then I'd leave. I never slept over. Not once. She also used to invite me to hang out with her and her friends, but at the time, I kept us a secret. I didn't tell any of my mates, and I didn't really want to be seen in public with her. I was weird about that. I liked sleeping in my own bed. I didn't want to open up. I didn't want that vulnerability—the vulnerability of falling asleep in another person's arms. I couldn't stomach it. Most men can't. And it's deeply unfortunate.

Beautiful, talented, and kind, she was and remains amazing. A real showstopper. She had this thick brown hair that fell like a waterfall right past her shoulders. And as a triathlete, she was built. She was funny, generous, and gave one of those Gatsby-like smiles, concentrating on you and lifting you up. She was really, really fucking cool. She wore very little makeup and only owned maybe like six dresses, all jet black. That's all she wore—black dresses. She had maybe one pair of heels and a bunch of flats. Her style was simple and elegant, charming and sophisticated in its minimalism.

I drunk-texted her a few times really dopey, lovey-dovey shit like "never change, Rockstar, you're awesome," and other things of the like. Only when I was really gone. Other than that, though, I don't think I gave an enormous amount of signaling that I was super into her. To much the same effect, I pretty much put off seeing her for the entire month of May when it came time to buckle down and study for exams. In the end I got the A's I wanted, but they came at a cost.

As to what exactly happened, there was no break. There was no definitive moment when we fought and broke up. My decision to boycott her for the month of May so that I could focus on my exams resulted, I think, in pushing her away a bit.

The guy she had dated for three years before me and who she had expected to give her the white dress and the ring, up and appeared on her doorstep with flowers one day in June, though. We had one of those phone calls where I was like, I'll give you your space if you want it, and I understand if you would prefer for me to not be in your life, even as friend. She insisted that she wanted me in her life as a friend, and I said okay.

Part of it also had to do with protecting the hedonistic tendencies that I so enjoy. I was twenty-one-years-old and a sophomore in college, keen on enjoying my youth and juggling flings as young men do. These were the golden years—whatever that means—the only four I had as an undergrad. And I wasn't about to give that up for a full-fledged relationship. Somehow, I came to internalize the belief that a relationship wouldn't go anywhere—that even if it was fun while it lasted, I might end up resenting her for locking me into monogamy at an inappropriate time and for infringing upon the sovereignty of my youth. I feared that maybe she would've ended up resenting me for hedonism, and that I would've been that guy, that cheating douche—the one that I loathe and never want to be. The dissolution of our relationship, in this way, came as a result of some weird self-fulfilling prophecy wherein I doomed it to fail before it even began by never really giving it a shot.

Do I regret not trying harder? Of course. She's getting married soon and moved to Los Angeles earlier this year. I've never been so happy for someone and carried around such a shattered heart at the same time. It's a weird feeling to confront your own hypocrisy. With me and my whole philosophy of embracing the excesses and the absolutes, of cloaking caution in clouds of exhaust, and running to the ends of the earth with ideas, people, passions, interests, and adventures, of taking things way too far just for the hell of it, I realize now that I probably should've opened up and given it a shot, if, for nothing else, just to see where it took me.

But in the end, I wasn't willing to give up everything else—the parties, the girls, the lost dawns, and the devil may care delight of life as a bachelor.

What I realize now is that I wouldn't have had to give up any of it. She would've just been another character on the stage.

So again, we return to the adage that underlay the story of Hanna: "*of all sad words of tongue or pen, The saddest are these: 'It might have been!'*"[29] If I had gone to Duke. If I hadn't fucked things up with Ava. What if. What if. What if. Life isn't a game of *What ifs*. Nor should it be.

Paul Arden got it right. "It's better to regret what you have done," he noted, "than what you haven't."[30]

29 John Greenleaf Whittier, "Maud Muller," 1856.

30 Paul Arden, *Whatever You Think Think the opposite* (London: Penguin Books, 2006).

CHAPTER XVII

MACALLAN

———

I learned far more in bars and gin-joints than I ever did at Princeton. Billy Joel's "Piano Man" strikes at the very heart of human interaction.[31] So too does pretty much every lyric from Kiss's "Strutter," a musical version of McInerney's *Bright Lights Big City*.[32,33]

In this beautiful and irreparably fucked up, yet nonetheless majestic, twenty-first century of ours, the battle between the sexes and the way camaraderie has come to exist is epitomized at the libation-serving establishment. Not to overemphasize the aspects of this shit too much, but if you go into a bar—any bar, at least any of the many I've spent my time in—you see the products of evolution, the very telos of western civilization in all its depravity.

Though I've visited many places, I know the most about New York City. Whether it's representative or not is up to you. But to me, it seems like the same fucking story wherever I go. The bars I frequent do, admittedly, attract a certain clientele,

---

31 Billy Joel, "Piano Man," single, Columbia. 1973.

32 Kiss, "Strutter," Track 1 on *Kiss*, Casablanca, 1974.

33 Jay McInerney, *Bright Lights, Big City* (London ; Oxford ; New York ; New Delhi ; Sydney: Bloomsbury, 2017), n.p.

but not one that is so insular as to preclude it from being representative. I think my fellow bar mates are, for the most part, just like everybody else—same stories, same issues, same drama, and same bullshit.

Details, of course, are interchangeable, but humans really aren't that complex. We run in circles, all of us, and the same ten to fifteen issues face us all. Of course, my delightful cynicism is sometimes put on hold when I meet somebody that knocks my socks off and baffles the shit out of me. That, of course, is always fun. It's a shock to the system, a shot in the dark, and a jolt awake. It's a reminder that I'm not as smart as I think I am. But, when you see different rounds of the same fight cycling through on repeat, you identify patterns, and it's not long before you've "seen it all." That's why I'm constantly searching out these shocking explosions of flavor, color, and excitement.

Without further ado, I'd like to introduce you to some of the most quintessential personalities of the bar.

THE SELF-PROCLAIMED PICKUP ARTIST:

You've got the boys who walk up to girls and try to hit on them like some kind of pickup artist. Let's be honest. We've all read that depraved and highly amusing account of Neil Strauss running around and trying to Genghis Khan himself into legend. The book I'm referring to, in case you're not familiar, is aptly entitled *The Game: Penetrating the Secret Society of Pickup Artists,* and, though journalistic in nature, is something of a manual on how to get laid.[34] I've read the thing, and I will say that it's fascinating.

---

34   Neil Strauss, *The Game: Undercover in the Secret Society of Pick-up Artists* (New York, N.Y.: It Books, 2005), n.p.

I was less interested in what Strauss was actually doing in the book than in his earnest belief that attraction was a science.

The book inspired a generation of hapless men to run around trying to talk to women by memorizing opening lines, employing attempts to undermine their self-worth with backhanded compliments and using all kinds of other "techniques."

Frankly, a lot of it was disgusting. But, I get it. There's the whole thrill-of-the-chase thing. And maybe some guys need structure in order to speak to women. Speaking to a beautiful woman or any woman who you don't know is, after all, terrifying. So, I do sympathize with the dude who feels like he needs some kind of advice on how to start a conversation.

The calculated responses and memorized retorts though seem inescapably inauthentic, disingenuous, and fake. The "playful" insults are also, sometimes, downright rude, bordering on cruel. I don't want to be a dick who says that any guy who uses the system is some cuck, loser. I sympathize enormously with the misfits, the guys who have a tough time. And if a memorized opener or whatever is enough to get a guy talking to a girl, that's fine. But be genuine. Be yourself. You can't live your whole life posturing.

THE FUCHBOI:
The next type is the fuchboi, a man of many masks. The most obvious version, played to the nines by Trevor Wallace in his videos, is the Supreme-sporting, beanie-in-the-summer-wearing frat boi.

They flex.
They insult.
They degrade.

They day-drink hard seltzers and Monster, and they have absolutely no respect for women. Fuchbois and fuchboish behavior needs to cut. Period.

THE FINANCE BRO:

We also, of course, have the finance bros. There are plenty of good men who work in finance, but they don't fall under the dominion of finance bro, even if they wear one of those God-awful Patagonia vests. I'm talking about Mr. Trader Guy. The guy who responds to "So, what do you do?" with "It's really complicated," falsely assuming that the girl wouldn't be able to understand.

It's more likely that she wouldn't care about your bitch work on Evercore's Forex desk, Preston.

The finance bro is earnestly convinced that the girl is lucky to be talking to him, thinking of himself as some investment she's gonna in him because of his current and future earning potential. He runs back to his buddies, post-rejection, giggling and referring to her as a bitch. That's no bueno either, amigo. Really, no bueno. You and your TUMI wallet and off-the-rack Loro Piana overcoat can fuck right off, Bradley.

THE TECH BRO:

Oh, boy. The java junkies are no picnic. In some cases, they're the worst of the worst. The finance bros, at least, are forced into polite social interaction in their client meetings. The tech bros suffer from what a call a L.O.N.T.S.I:.

A lack of non tech-related social interaction.

Silicon Valley incarnate.

Now, it should be noted that I do not wish for you to conflate the tech bro with a person who works in tech. The tech bro is a very specific subspecies of fuchboi. As he likely does not know how to speak with girls, instead of just being the cute, shy, and geeky guy that would probably be kind of loveable, he showboats as a colossal douchebag—referring to women as bitches, throwing down his newly acquired metal credit card on the table, wearing designer tee shirts with enormous logos, and doing stupid amounts of blow that he can't handle.

THE AWKWARD CHARLIE:
The awkward Charlie is generally normal, but shy. He's probably in a band, or maybe not. But, at a minimum, he loves music.

THE NICE GUY:
Of course, then, there are the nice guys. The guys who start genuine conversations and don't go into an interaction with the explicit intention of getting laid. If it happens, it happens, but it shouldn't be the intent. Maybe, you'll actually get to know somebody and share a good conversation. People hook up—I regularly hook up—and that's fine. But there should be some humanity in it.

Bars have taught me far more than the Ivy League. Other than the catalogue of male characters, the libation-serving establishment has taught me about social dynamics.

THE WOMEN ARE IN CHARGE:
Whether they admit it or not, on some level, men spend most of their lives seeking out the validation and approval of women. This isn't a bad thing. It's just something I've observed. And maybe it's wrong, but I doubt it because I've seen far too much of it.

The girls, the ones who really know how to work it, wrap men around their fingers and melt them into puddles of submission. It's not about sex or sex appeal. It's about the underlying dynamic. A smart gal knows full-well that men are keen to please, and she withholds her approval, using a push-and-pull technique to lure in the man. Again, this isn't a bad thing. The girls that figure out how to do this well are typically winners. I know this because they're some of my best friends.

On that note, just to be clear, this has absolutely nothing to do with using one's sexuality to advance their career. That's not what I'm getting at, and I don't want this being misconstrued. I'm talking about social dynamics, not about horse-trading.

THE DICK-MEASURING CONTEST NEVER ENDS:

There's also the never-ending dick measuring contest between guys at the bar. It's both between dudes who don't know each other, and it's between friends. Everything from talking about their high school glory days, to snorting more expensive cocaine, to the brands they wear, the cars they drive, the art they buy, and the titles they hold. Some real Patrick Bateman shit. The ceaseless dick-measuring is an unfortunate byproduct of evolution, and it's ubiquitous.

FUNDAMENTALS OF PARTY ETIQUETTE:

First and foremost, bars taught me to handle my liquor. Secondly, bars have taught me how to talk to people; because, who doesn't like talking in a bar? And most of all, bars taught me to respect hard work.

The barmaids and the bouncers of our world deserve a fucking medal, especially those tasked with manning Manhattan's finest establishments.

Bouncers have to deal with all kinds of infamy: fights, refusal to pay bills, spousal violence, fake IDs, and teens trying to sneak in (as if I wasn't totally this kid, though I was typically successful). And sometimes, they've got to do it in the freezing cold. New York City, after all, can have pretty fucking arctic temperatures.

Then, there are the barmaids and barmen, negotiating all kinds of weird social interactions, soberly (at least for the most part) watching patrons get piss drunk, and staying long after the four o'clock in the morning lights come on to clean up and shut things down.

If I can give you any advice, it's this: make friends with the barmaids and the bouncers. Ask them about themselves, take a genuine interest, and build a relationship. While they may be there to serve you, it's always good to show some fucking humanity. You'll get expedited entry and free drinks as a result, though that really shouldn't be the motivation. Treat them well, tip them generously, and actually get to know them. They've seen some ridiculous shit to be sure, and they've all got one or two war stories that they're more than willing to share.

The bar teaches you how to observe, to interact, to negotiate, to navigate, to love, to forget, to cry, and to ride on. It's the place you go to forgive and forget, to love and to learn, to share silence with strangers, and to pleasantly plunge into the abyss and to swim back up to the surface.

If you ever see me in a bar, come and say hey. There is no such thing as a stranger—only a friend whom you haven't met yet. I saw that on a plaque in a ski lodge once.

By the way, the entirety of this chapter's first draft was written during a three-hour plane ride on my phone. Welcome to the twenty-first century, bitch.

CHAPTER XVIII

JACK

———

Sometimes in life, you meet somebody or stumble across something that changes your life for the better: a jolt of energy, a shot in the dark, a lightning bolt shock to the heart that wakes you up to something that has been in your life the whole time. For me, that person was Jack.

Princeton had rubbed off on me hard, and I all but had that proverbial suit molded onto me like papier-mâché. It wasn't just the incessant procession of jobs, internships, and prestige (think, Soho House and its equivalents in all realms of life). It was everything. I had begun measuring myself and my value by what I thought I was *supposed* to do. I was a sheep, a gray-flannel suit-wearing cuck. I needed to channel my inner Kanye, and Jack, who I stumbled upon by accident, helped me get there.

It all started at Otto's Shrunken Head, a dive bar down on the Lower East Side whose door was manned by the legendary Jack Schaffer. He was short and stout with a healthy port-belly that had inhaled its fair share of beer, coke, whiskey, and everything else humanely available, a big white beard, a bunch of tats and a bunch of rings, a vest with a shit-ton of pockets in it that contained the secrets of the universe, black leather boots, and a huge pair of Dr. TJ Eckleburg's.[35]

He had that classic Bronx Italian voice that you know and love. He'd probably seen the most obscene and ungodly things in his day, but that's another story. There's a story about him in *The New York Times*, I think. The man is a legend. He worked with the Grateful Dead for years and saw all kinds of debauchery, I'm sure, in his time. Now, he books bands for Otto's Shrunken Head.

When I sauntered on up to the bar, I ordered a bourbon and coke and minded my business. The bartender—whatever her name was—had large, rotund mammories that she had pushed up under a low-cut top. She was covered in tattoos and had a pretty face complete with black bangs, a nose ring, and a spunky attitude. She was Australian or South African, and she had a twin brother. The reason I remember this is because I asked her if they were identical, and she grabbed her breasts and shot back, "Maybe, but he doesn't have these." Then she winked at me, licked her lips is a very lascivious manner, and cackled affectionately.

Shortly thereafter, Jack approached and started trying to make conversation. Frankly, I think he just wanted to make me feel cool. He was the type of guy that had drank, snorted, and fucked so much in his day that, like a pair of leather pants on the Sunset Strip, by the end of the decade, he really had seen it all. He had all these stories to tell, to transmit, and to share. And because most of his friends were dead, forgotten, or otherwise gone, he pawned them off on young padawans like me at the bar. That's all just

---

35 Reference to F. Scott Fitzgerald, *The Great Gatsby* (Richmond, Surrey: Alma Classics, 2017), n.p.

musing and speculation. Maybe he liked my rings. Who the fuck actually knows?

Somewhere in the conversation, he started telling me about all the bands he booked for Otto's, which had live band performances almost every night of the week that started at ten or eleven o'clock in the evening.

"You should come by," he suggested in a hoarse, grumbling voice full of power. "You seem like a rock and roller."

"How do you expect anybody to show up on a weeknight."

"What'd ya mean?"

"Well, most people have work in the morning."

"Kid," he chuckled, "not everybody has the kind of jobs you're thinking of. Not everybody works a nine-to-five."

Jack was right. Not everybody worked white collar jobs where they punched in and punched out. There were creatives, artists, rebels, entrepreneurs, and lovers of music out there. There were even the nine-to-fivers who made it work because they didn't have any other choice. The set begins and ends when the set begins and ends. And if that means you lose a few hours of sleep to see your favorite bands, it's a small price to pay.

At Lawrenceville and Princeton, I developed tunnel vision. In high school, the singular purpose of my existence was to bullshit my way into Princeton, Harvard, Stanford, or Yale. And at a tremendous cost to myself, my relationships, my intellectual curiosity, and my personal growth, I did. At Princeton, my singular goal was to social climb—into the right fraternities, eating clubs, and jobs. I neglected relationships, meaningful experiences, and academic rigor in favor of the social ladder.

For a six-year period (four years of Lawrenceville and two of Princeton), I more or less lost my way. I was curious, excited, and used to have this spark of wonder in me. When I lived in Antibes and Paris, I really did race against the trains.

I was carefree, fun, and excited about the world. I loved reading and meeting new people. And then, the college application process set me on a path that sucked all those vibrant colors out of me. The never-ending life-pervading rat race had done me dirty. The sheep had won.

This is not to say that I didn't have bouts of clarity. Paris round dos and Jordan were two such examples. The brief period of time in which I turned down five Ivies and committed to Duke was another. But, they were punctuated and rare. They weren't my life. They were inside of life's parentheses.

Jack jolted me out of the rat race. Investment banking simply was not my cup of gin. And, it was time I started thinking for myself again.

CHAPTER XIX

THE SAGA OF THE SUNDAY NIGHT ESCAPADES

—

Then there was Marc, and the saga of the Sunday night escapades. Marc, a friend from the Paris years, had one of those great, baritone laughs that came from deep within the chest. Having just come back from Europe, he had a twenty-hour layover in New York City, and I intended to put those hours to work!

He got in sometime on a Sunday afternoon. First and foremost, I ordered him to nap.

"But I'm not tired," he protested.

"It doesn't matter," I retorted. "You're napping."

And nap he did. He was going to need energy for the long stretch we had ahead of us.

When he was done napping, we went out and watched *Fast & Furious Presents: Hobbs & Shaw* in theaters.[36] I'm a

---

36   *Fast & Furious Presents: Hobbs & Shaw*, directed by David Leitch, Universal Pictures, 2019.

die-hard *Fast and Furious* fan, so there wasn't a snowball's chance in hell I was about to miss the film. I was seriously pissed at the producers for bringing science fiction elements into the film, but I forgave them on account of the plentiful portion of action porn they generously served.

Immediately after seeing the movie, I made the executive decision that we were to go swimming at the pool in my gym. We began walking there in earnest, but alas, the pool was closed. After heading back on to my apartment, we recharged, getting locked, loaded, and ready for action.

To save time on dinner, rather than blow two hours on a sit-down jousting match with our taste buds, I took him to Papaya King. Hands down, best hot dog in the city. No other hot dog comes close.

Next, we made sure to put on the most ridiculous outfits that we could find because it was a Sunday night and we wanted to go out and the place to go out on Sunday nights is Bushwick. I wore all white everything, and Marc sported this wild animal print silk shirt I lent him that I had picked up at a thrift shop. And with that, we mounted our thirty-minute Brooklyn-bound Uber and hurled ourselves off into the night. Along the way, I read obscure passages from my favorite novels out loud, and we opened the windows and screamed like hyenas.

When we finally got to House of Yes, it was, to our dismay, closed. That was probably one of the only Sunday nights that whole summer when House of Yes was closed. And, their website had said they were open. But, alas, 'twasn't. So, on we marched. We'd come this far, and we weren't about to turn back. Next, we trotted to Elsewhere. And wouldn't you know it, Elsewhere was closed too.

Sure, there were other bars on Johnson Avenue we could've slipped into. But they were quiet, tame, and markedly dead. And it's not like I had the time or inclination to book it all the way over to Skinny D's (The Skinny Dennis). We didn't come out for a few lonely drinks with the bartender. We needed the big guns, the loud-speakers, and the tropical themes. We needed to explore something new and hangout with the degenerates, rascals, acrobats, dancers, and crazies who had no problem going out on a Sunday night. We needed Bossa Nova.

After a hopscotch and skedaddle, we found ourselves at Bossa Nova Civic Club. Before going in, I lit a cigarette and watched the strange comings and goings of the place. First, I saw a backpack-sporting high school girl, who couldn't have been older than eighteen, walk up to the bouncer matter-of-factly and hand over her license.

"This says you're eighteen," he chuckled, clearly amused at the fact that she hadn't even shown him a fake.

"Yeah but..."

"Look. I get it. My brother tries the same shit. But to be frank, there are plenty of other bars around here that won't give a fuck."

"Yeah, you're right. It was worth a shot."

The peppiness of this girl astounded me. It was kind of hilarious. She was very clearly underage and she didn't try to hide it. Props to her for the honesty.

Then, there were some French dudes outside who I over-heard and conversed with. I don't remember if I just started speaking in French or if I went over and pretended not to have a lighter—always a fantastic way to strike up a conversation. We chatted for a minute and then all of us headed inside.

Enter: Bossa Nova. Walk through a hallway decorated with all kinds of wild neon prints. See that the dance floor is somewhat crowded. Go to the Bar. Order Drinks. See more

French people inside. Say hello. Give them handshakes and fist bumps. Look at the guy in front of you wearing one of those stupid fedoras. Judge him. Go to pay with your credit card and be told there's a minimum. Get a little annoyed about this because you already ordered two drinks. Consider ordering a third and giving it to somebody as a gift. Realize this isn't some swanky-fucking-meatpacking bar where people buy drinks for strangers. Ask Marc for cash. He ponies it up, and you pay for the drinks while tipping the bartender.

Take a picture with Marc. It's good. You're glad you took it.

Stroll on over to cut up the dance floor. And cut up the dance floor you do. You cut that shit hard like you're a pair of scissors gliding down a page.

Lose Marc. Find Marc and tell him that you guys should move to the front of the dance floor. Soon, you're tired, really tired. It's time for some good old-fashioned pick-me-up, but not the powdery kind. Why is there no Sunset Strip in New York City?

Head to the bar with Marc and order Mate. Drink it. It tastes neither good nor bad. Tell Marc to remind you that by the end of the night, you really, really need to get one of the Mate shirts that the bartender is wearing that you saw one of the other patrons buy.

Make the executive decision that it's time to yeet out back home. Do so, of course, only after getting that shirt. Buy shirt first. Leave. Mount a chariot, stand on top of it, and surf our way over the bridge and back into the place they call Manhattan.

Go to the Carl Schurz Park on East End Avenue. Sit by the water. Talk about life and drink in the view.

Wakeup at nine o'clock in the morning on little sleep ready to attack the day. Pawn Marc off on a friend, who has agreed to show him the *Camp Exhibit* at the Met, while you run errands.

Laugh when you hear that Marc missed his flight because he spent far too long at the *Camp Exhibit*.

What is there to take away from all this? Go out, even if it's a Sunday and nothing is open and you have shit to do in the morning. *Carpe*-fucking-*noctem*. It's not like I did this on the regular. Marc was an irregular guest in town, meaning I had an ethical obligation to show him around. When shit hits the fan because the first two or three places you wanted to go are no-gos, you just gotta ride on into the night, surf the moonlit waves, and see where they take you.

CHAPTER XX

SHOWERS, WHISKEY, & ALBANIAN MOBSTERS

——

I first met Karina at the Brandy Library located way downtown. I was seeing a show nearby with some people of whom I was not the greatest fan, and I thought I'd have a drink or two beforehand to lubricate myself into easier social interaction with the head-assed ruffians I was to cavort with thereafter.

Shortly into enjoying my Moscow mule, which I ordered despite my general rule against drinking syrupy cocktails, I encountered Karina with a group of her friends.

"How's the vodka? I prefer mine straight" she purred.

It seemed like a rather cartoonish thing to say, a line she'd thought up to impress me with her heavy drinking skills.

Immediately, though, she ordered two shots. One for her, and for her "new American friend." I'm always a fan of free drinks. We hung out for a bit with one thing leading to another, and all of a sudden a couple of nights later, we were having dinner at some Spanish tapas bar in Hell's Kitchen. We went on a few more dates and started hooking up somewhere along the way.

Life then got in the way with the distractions of the Fourth of July, an impromptu trip to Chile, and my attendance of Lollapalooza Chicago and Electric Zoo. So, in the end, Karina and I didn't hangout for like six weeks. Then, a few nights before I was due to book it back to Princeton, I reached out and set up a dinner.

First, we went to some French restaurant in Midtown. Then, she insisted that we go hangout in the park, which I thought was an absurd and horrible idea. You don't go hangout in Central Park at night. But she was adamant and insistent, so I said fuck it and to the park we went. After the park, we went back to my apartment and had sex first on my desk then in my bed.

Fast forward to post-park, post-hook up, and in my apartment around two o'clock in the morning: we were spooning. Around two-thirty in the morning, she began telling me how her uncle is heavily involved with the Albanian mob. She announced casually that the reason she had to flee New Zealand and Azerbaijan was because men with guns had come looking for things, pointing those guns at her and her brothers, and ultimately forcing her dad to sign papers of some kind. While I appreciated her opening up to me, I was also rather *shooketh*. So much for pillow talk.

After about an hour of cuddling, she got up and decidedly announced her intention to shower. I got her a towel and went back to bed. About five minutes into her shower, she began calling my name. There she was, peaking her head out the bathroom door and asking me to join her.

Beaming, I ran into the other room to disrobe. And that's when I saw it: a battery of missed notifications including calls, voicemails, texts.

This is where shit started getting scary. There were missed calls from some angry Albanian dude and missed texts from a seemingly angrier Albanian woman. Apparently, Karina didn't tell her uncle, the mobster, and the mobster's girlfriend who she was staying with in New York and that she wouldn't be coming home that night. But, how the fuck had they gotten my phone number? How did they even know who I was? It was then that my stomach sank, and I played out the worst possible scenario in my mind. What if this was all some sort of depraved kinky game in which she had texted her uncle so that he could come to my apartment and kill me after finding me in the shower with his niece?

As this scenario plays out in my mind, I also remember that there's a gorgeous girl who just asked me to shower with her. A real twenty-first century *Catch-22*.[37]

Maybe it was the whiskey or maybe it was the anxiety of going back to school, but a paralyzing fear that her uncle and some mob goons were going to burst in washed over me, and I ultimately refused to get in the shower with her.

She was pissed that I wouldn't join her, but she initially refused to explain what was going on. Eventually, embarrassed, she explained that she shared an iCloud account with her friend. When she didn't come home, her brother asked the friend if the friend knew where Karina was. The friend said maybe with this guy (me). The brother gave the number and contact info to the uncle and his girlfriend. And subsequently, they called, texted, and left me voicemails. The whole thing was weird—too weird.

We dozed off, and the following morning, I awoke to Dyson-grade suction.

Frankly, it's horrid of me to even be writing this story. But, what the hell?

---

37 Joseph Heller, *Catch-22* (London: Random House, 2003), n.p.

CHAPTER XXI

PISCOLA

———

Who knows where a story really ends or begins? I don't think we're ever at the start or finish of anything. It's all just one cacophonous succession of events. She says one thing. I say another, and suddenly we're in Paris, Jordan, Darwin, or at The Rainbow in Hollywood. Life is not so much of a book as it is a web, an internet, a collection of interwoven events bonding us together in a foxtrot with the stars.

If there's any place to bring an unfinished story to a close, though, maybe it's Chile. In August of 2019, I found myself there on a five-day odyssey of sorts. Authentic Chilean barbecue with a bunch of former naval pilots, mid-summer skiing and beaching in the same forty-eight hours, getting rejected at the Argentinian border, and disconnecting the gas pipe to our car in a national park after off-roading were all rolled up into a ball of *what the fuck?*

Chile was sandwiched between two mind-bending music festivals of fear, loathing, and fun. Lollapalooza Chicago and Electric Zoo, more specifically, stood as firm placeholders bookending the Chile affair in my mind. Perhaps, it is for that reason that I remember it fondly as being a punctuated succession of madness in between those two distinctly long and wild bouts of craziness.

Since one of my boys was living in Chile for the summer, I decided it fitting and appropriate to accept his invitation to come down for a week and see how they did things. So off I went, jettisoning myself into a world I knew little about.

On one of the first days, we met the legendary Mateo. He was a friend of a friend of a friend, or something like that, and somehow, I ended up meeting him and some mutual friends of ours for lunch at some swanky Chilean restaurant. We dined, drank Pisco, exchanged stories, and laughed about girls and cars, and the rest of it. Immediately after lunch, Felipe announced that he was having a barbecue at his place that night and that I was invited.

There was no sit-down dinner. They just put a shit ton of juicy, bloody, delicious Chilean meat on the outdoor barbeque that they fired into edible condition. All thick and succulent, the meat options included steak, lamb, sausage, beef, pork, and veal. Frankly, I didn't know what I was eating, but I didn't care. Sometimes, it's best not to ruin things by asking questions that have answers you don't really care to know. The meal was orgasmic, a delectably sexual experience. The warm, thick, and perfectly textured flesh covered in viscous blood, juices, and sweat alarmed the senses to the fact that this was something special. Mateo mentioned casually that he had marinated some of that shit for four full days.

The high level of hospitality I experienced at Felipe's barbeque was unprecedented. While I've always been charming and likable, I'd never experienced graciousness so sincerely displayed to me as it was by Mateo.

Here he was, taking a stranger into his home and casually introducing me to his army of old buddies, business associates, and family members. There was absolutely nothing transactional about this—a refreshing change from New York City, Los Angeles, and Princeton. He rioted against the evolutionary impulse in favor of decency, and he did all of this without thinking twice.

At one point, he told me that he and his air force buddies were brothers. I laughed, thinking wrongly that they were just screwing with me. *Mais, non*, they were.

At one point when he was on his third glass of Pisco, Mateo pointed to his air force buddies and told me just how close they were. They were real brothers, he explained, because back when they were in flight school, they lived in a little cabin in the mountains that was so fucking freezing all the time that they'd huddle together for warmth when they slept. It wasn't just some story to impress the transplanted New Yorkers. It was about survival. They huddled to avoid death from Hypothermia and doing so bonded the shit out of them.

In some ways, the whole Mateo affair brought me back to Antibes: the cultural exchange, the mingling, the interplay of new and old, and the cross-generational cutting. It was different, but, of course, it was the same. Our interests, desires, hopes, and dreams, regardless of who or where we are, are more or less the same. Ethnicity, religion, and country of origin don't change that. There's something carnal, whole, pure, and beautiful about interacting with what's considered to be the other. Because, at the end of the day, through the crying and the laughing, the fucking and the fighting, the betting and the folding, you realize that a lot of these intangible experiences transcend the individual. Humans, at least in my experience, aren't really all that different. It's the same story, told about a thousand different ways.

The following day, we booked it down to Puerto Natales—the southernmost city in Chile. Icy, windy, and very fucking cold is the only way to describe what the weather was like down there. It was certainly a hell of a change from weather at Lollapalooza and the Electric Zoo.

There was an abandoned, in-ground skate park next to our hotel. One day, I strapped on my ski helmet, threw on my goggles, cranked "Kickstart My Heart" by Mötley Crüe, and ran around the skate park on foot, climbing up the walls like some sort of wannabe-Spiderman freak. [38] Anybody who saw me must have thought I had a few screws loose.

I remember seeing some of the most beautiful glaciers in the world, without question.

While in Puerto Natales, we tried to drive to Argentina for a good steak dinner, whereupon we were rejected entry as it is apparently illegal to leave the country with a rental car. Another time, we broke down our rental car in a national park while off-roading. It took us nearly an hour to reconnect the gas pipe, which blasted thick, disgusting fluid all over my shirt.

We also went bungee jumping on that trip. It was some beat-to-shit crane that was probably bolted improperly into the earth. There was pretty much no vetting process at all, other than giving him fake passport numbers and cash, and I couldn't understand what the man's instructions asked of us because I didn't speak Spanish. The one thing I did understand, though, is that once the crane had carried me out to the little platform from which I was to jump, I was not to look down. When on the platform, I began looking down

---

38 Mötley Crüe, "Kickstart my Heart," track 5 on Dr. Feelgood, Elektra Records, 1989.

at the rocky enclosure below, and the guy quickly started yelling at me in Spanish to look up.

What he was getting at, I think, is that if you look down, your body won't let you hurl yourself off a cliff toward certain death. So, you just have to look across, straight ahead, level-eyed, and then tres, dos, uno, and off you jump. It's a rush faster than anything you've ever felt before—skiing, running, driving—nothing is faster than that face first plunge. Then, the rope gets taut as you're catapulted up into the sky, causing an orgasm where you first feel a sense of relief and then simultaneously feel a need to projectile vomit and realize that no, you did not, in fact, die.

What was the most hilarious part about bungee jumping for me? I was wearing fucking leather loafers. In leather loafers, black moto jeans with the ribbing above the knees, and a turquoise t-shirt, I was dressed to go to a club. In fact, I think I was at one—or maybe it was a bar—the night before.

Bungee jumping off some rickety-shit crane in the Chilean mountains was, for me, akin to fucking Valeriya all of those years ago. When an opportunity presents itself to you, seize it. Seize the shit out of it. Life isn't a journey following a linear progression toward some teleological end. It's a collection of moments. Seize them.

All the social-laddering and prestige-seeking of boarding school and Princeton and the rest was a world apart. It was, in many ways, a world that I'd left behind. Chile for me was to Princeton what Paris had been to Lawrenceville. But, at the same time, it was more.

Chile was the rest of my life. No more bullshit. No more noise. No more living off of the parentheses—subsisting in monotony punctuated by bouts of exciting breaks. Rather than lay back and think of England as a fusillade of grocery shopping and insurance claims and daytime TV overran me, I resolved in Chile to take a stand. Bungee jumping, skiing, off-roading, and running around skate rinks was to be my life.

I will continue to forge my own destiny, regardless of whatever is written in the stars. My business is one of chucking color into the bland, doughy monotony of everyday life, erupting like a Jackson Pollock on the scene.

Chile became a model for how I wanted to live. It was my canvas, and I was going to paint it. Bright, beautiful, and however the fuck I so chose.

CHAPTER XXII

THE NIGHT BEFORE
THE MORNING AFTER

———

It's always gonna be the night before the morning after: the spectacular promise of a world unknown—the thick, creamy canvas of an Arabian night. All I can do, all any of us can do, is charge forth and conquer. Dare to dream, to fall, to dance, to laugh, to cry, to feel, and to share. Our days are numbered, and we live on borrowed time. That magical set of parentheses that slides between dawn and dusk—that's really all we have. The only thing that's certain in this world is that the morning will eventually come. And when you look back on the night before—that golden warping of space time—I hope you're surprised, by yourself, and by all the other actors on the stage.

At twenty-one, I've chosen to live my life as a writer and a rockstar, a poet and a matador, a sailor and a pilot. The excesses and the absolutes, the wild adventures, and the long treks home—that's where I belong. I've found nobility in the rejection of a blank canvas, a vanilla void.

I hope you find whatever it is you're looking for out there, and when you do, I hope a firestorm riots against the great white stars of the beach and the night, infringing forcefully on the sovereignty of the ever black.

It's time for this cub scout to check out. I've got dances to dance, songs to sing, words to write, hugs to give, and toasts to make. The words, though, at least at this point, have reached their limit. Is there a hell of a lot more left to say? Of course. But not right now. Thanks for humoring me through the last however many pages.

APPENDIX

CHAPTER I: SOMETHING LIKE AN INTRODUCTION

CHAPTER II: ANTIBES

CHAPTER III: VALERIYA

CHAPTER IV: KATHERINE BLACK

CHAPTER V: THE BOARDING SCHOOL YEARS
Ferris Bueller's Day Off. Directed by John Hughes. Paramount Pictures, 1986.

Fitzgerald, F. Scott. *The Great Gatsby.* Richmond, Surrey: Alma Classics, 2017.

Kālidāsa and Ashok Sinha. *Shakuntala: A Play on the Birth of Bharat.* Bloomington, IN: Xlibris, 2011.

Salinger, Jerome David. *The Catcher in the Rye.* Harmondsworth: Penguin Books, 2019.

Shakespeare, William, Jesse M. Lander, and Kevin Stanton. *Macbeth.* New York: Sterling Signature, 2012.

CHAPTER VI: MR. BOLLINGER
Kipling, Rudyard. "If," c1895.

Shakespeare, William, John Gilbert, and Ned Halley. *Julius Ceasar.* Complete & unabridged. ed. London: Macmillan Collector's Library, 2016.

CHAPTER VII: PARIS
Potts, Rolf. *Vagabonding: An Uncommon Guide to the Art of Long-term World Travel.* 2016 ed. New York: Ballantine Books, 2016.

Richardson, John. "CRIMES OF THE ART." *Vanity Fair,* April 5, 2012. Accessed October 1, 2020.

CHAPTER VIII: HANNA
Whittier, John Greenleaf. "Maud Muller." 1856.

CHAPTER IX: AN ANGRY BEDOUIN AND THE WARM JORDANIAN SUN

CHAPTER X: BULLETS AND BALLGAMES
McInerney, Jay. *Bright Lights, Big City*. London ; Oxford ; New York ; New Delhi ; Sydney: Bloomsbury, 2017.

CHAPTER XI: CRUMPET-EATING LIMEYS
Dunston Checks in. Directed by Ken Kwapis. 20th Century Fox, 1996.

CHAPTER XII: HOW I GOT INTO PRINCETON
Newport, Cal. *How to Be a High School Superstar: A Revolutionary Plan to Get into College by Standing out (without Burning Out)*. New York: Broadway Books, 2010.

Office of Communications. "Princeton offers admission to 6.1 percent of Class of 2021 applicants." Princeton University. Last modified March 2, 2017.

The Dark Knight Rises, directed by Christopher Nolan, Warner Bros Pictures, 2012.

The Dark Knight Rises (Soundtrack). Composed by Hans Zimmer. WaterTower Music. 2012

The Fate of the Furious. Directed by F. Gary Gray, Universal Pictures, 2017.

CHAPTER XIII: THE COLLEGE ESSAYS I NEVER SUBMITTED
Breaking Bad. Season 5, episode 16, "Felina." Performed by Bryan Cranston. Vince Gilligan. Aired September 29, 2013, on AMC.

CHAPTER XIV: COLLEGE
Bennett, Jane. *Vibrant Matter: A Political Ecology of Things*. Durham: Duke University Press, 2010.

Berlant, Lauren Gail. *Cruel Optimism*. Durham: Duke University Press, 2011.

Duke University Press. "Vibrant Matter A Political Ecology of Things." Duke University Press. Accessed October 20, 2020. https://www.dukeupress.edu/vibrant-matter.

Gossip Girl. Season 3, episode 22, "Last Tango, Then Paris." Directed by J. Miller Tobin. Written by Josh Safran and Stephanie Savage. Aired May 17, 2010, on The CW.

Mounk, Yascha. "What an Audacious Hoax Reveals About Academia." *The Atlantic*, October 5, 2018. Accessed October 1, 2020.

CHAPTER XV: CORPORATE CONTACTS
Orwell, George. *Animal Farm: A Fairy Story*. New York, NY: Signet Classics, 2020.

CHAPTER XVI: HENDRICK'S & TONIC
Arden, Paul. *Whatever You Think Think the Opposite*. London: Penguin Books, 2006.

CHAPTER XVII: MACALLAN

Billy Joel, "Piano Man," single, Columbia. 1973.

Kiss, "Strutter," Track 1 on *Kiss*, Casablanca, 1974.

McInerney, Jay. *Bright Lights, Big City*. London ; Oxford ; New York ; New Delhi ; Sydney: Bloomsbury, 2017.

Strauss, Neil. *The Game: Undercover in the Secret Society of Pick-up Artists*. New York, N.Y.: It Books, 2005.

CHAPTER XVIII: JACK

Fitzgerald, F. Scott. *The Great Gatsby*. Richmond, Surrey: Alma Classics, 2017.

CHAPTER XIX: THE SAGA OF THE SUNDAY NIGHT ESCAPADES

Fast & Furious Presents: Hobbs & Shaw. Directed by David Leitch. Universal Pictures, 2019.

CHAPTER XX: SHOWERS, WHISKEY, & ALBANIAN MOBSTERS

Heller, Joseph. *Catch-22*. London: Random House, 2003.

CHAPTER XXI: PISCOLA

Mötley Crüe, "Kickstart My Heart," track five on *Dr. Feelgood*, Elektra Records, 1989.

CHAPTER XXII: THE NIGHT BEFORE THE MORNING AFTER

Lightning Source UK Ltd.
Milton Keynes UK
UKHW020101211120
373778UK00003B/5/J